T0006621

Praise for *Container Magic*

"This book stands out in the crowd—it is clear, practical, and invites us to have fun while still being effective magic-workers. Go get it! You need this on your shelf and in your magical hands." —**H. Byron Ballard, author of *Roots, Branches & Spirits* and *Seasons of a Magical Life***

"Charity Bedell writes in a clear and easily understood manner. Her explanations of how not only container magic works but also magic itself are precise and easily practiced. I would recommend this to be in any beginner or novice witch's library." —**Cassandra Campbell, host of the *Arcane Conjurings* podcast**

"Containers are one of my favorite ways to work; Charity did a great job explaining the differences in the works. This is a wonderful read." —**Starr Casas, bestselling author of *Old Style Conjure***

"Charity is a gifted writer, and this book is her present to the magical world. Not stopping at the basics, she affords the reader comprehensive instructions and explanations for container magic." —**Kenya T. Coviak, host of the *My Magical Cottagecore Life* podcast**

"Charity Bedell offers up a bewitching brew of some of the most venerable magic of the past and blends it with her own magical sensibilities … I deeply appreciate how Charity has laid these enchanting tools out for the practitioner to start using right away!" —**Christian Day, author of** *The Witches' Book of the Dead*

"This wise and approachable spellbook expertly summarizes these practices and so much more … Drawing both on European witchcraft and southern Conjure traditions, Charity weaves a tome of animistic wisdom appropriate for magickal practitioners of all varieties." —**Raven Digitalis, author of** *Esoteric Empathy*

"Clear, concise, and loaded with insight that a witch at any level can benefit from. Bedell weaves technique and tradition into a thoroughly modern approach to witchcraft … Bedell brings these practices into the modern age with the poise and insight of a master." —**Devin Hunter, bestselling author of** *Modern Witch*

"This is a wonderfully well-written and enjoyable little book that is just chock full of material that covers an often-overlooked area of magical practice. From guidance on the most beneficial containers and magical correspondences to a delightful set of spells and even exercises to help you further your experience, this book offers it all." —**Mama Sha', swamp witch and owner of Inexplicable Things Apothecary**

"Charity deftly weaves the strands of her own training and practice together to create this very complete exploration of container magic. She has a nod to the formularies and spell books of old but applies her magic to today's world. You'll learn a lot from *Container Magic.*" —**Christopher Penczak, bestselling author of the Temple of Witchcraft series**

"A compelling and powerful read ... Well-researched. Well-sourced. A spellbinding book filled with magical lore and spells that promises to become a classic among classics used by beginner witches and elders alike." —**Shawn Robbins, author/coauthor of *The Good Witch's Guide*, *Wiccapedia*, and *The Witch's Way***

"Charity has great insight and wisdom in her book ... She makes it easy and fun to read and it draws you in immediately upon opening to the first page. A book I would recommend for anyone who is interested in learning magick or who has already been practicing for many years." —**Darcie Vélez, founder and high priestess of Temple of Diana**

"Charity Bedell makes use of a whole variety of methods to create, consecrate, bless, and activate different types of vessels ... Well-resourced and teaches you how to use the energies of magic for different purposes in an easy-to-follow way." —**Elhoim Leafar, author of *The Magical Art of Crafting Charm Bags***

Container
Magic

About the Author

Charity L. Bedell (Maine), also known as Loona Wynd, is the coauthor of The Good Witch's Guide series and *The Wiccapedia Spell Deck*. She has studied Conjure with Starr Casas and Feri with Veedub, and she is initiated in the Temple Tradition. Bedell has written for *The Witches' Almanac* and *Kindred Spirit Magazine*, and she has presented at festivals such as WitchCon2020.

CHARITY L. BEDELL

CONTAINER MAGIC

SPELLCRAFT USING SACHETS, BOTTLES, POPPETS & JARS

LLEWELLYN PUBLICATIONS
WOODBURY, MINNESOTA

FIRST EDITION
Second Printing, 2023

All the quotes and passages from the Bible in this book are from the New King James Version.
Book design by Christine Ha
Cover design by Cassie Willett

Llewellyn Publications is a registered trademark of Llewellyn Worldwide Ltd.

Library of Congress Cataloging-in-Publication Data
Names: Bedell, Charity (Witch), author.
Title: Container magic : spellcraft using sachets, bottles, poppets & jars / by Charity Bedell.
Description: First edition. | Woodbury, MN : Llewellyn Worldwide ltd, 2022. | Includes bibliographical references. | Summary: "Featuring more than 100 spells for mojo bags, poppets, talismans, jars, and other enchanted containers, this is the spell book you've always wanted"--Provided by publisher.
Identifiers: LCCN 2022046174 (print) | LCCN 2022046175 (ebook) | ISBN 9780738772615 (paperback) | ISBN 9780738772684 (ebook) Subjects: LCSH: Incantations.
Classification: LCC BF1558 .B44 2022 (print) | LCC BF1558 (ebook) | DDC
 133.4/4--dc23/eng/20221116
 LC record available at https://lccn.loc.gov/2022046174
 LC ebook record available at https://lccn.loc.gov/2022046175

Llewellyn Worldwide Ltd. does not participate in, endorse, or have any authority or responsibility concerning private business transactions between our authors and the public.

 All mail addressed to the author is forwarded but the publisher cannot, unless specifically instructed by the author, give out an address or phone number.

 Any internet references contained in this work are current at publication time, but the publisher cannot guarantee that a specific location will continue to be maintained. Please refer to the publisher's website for links to authors' websites and other sources.

Llewellyn Publications
A Division of Llewellyn Worldwide Ltd.
2143 Wooddale Drive
Woodbury, MN 55125-2989
www.llewellyn.com

Printed in the United States of America

Other Books by Charity L. Bedell

The Good Witch's Guide:
A Modern-Day Wiccapedia of Magickal Ingredients and Spells
(cowritten with Shawn Robbins, Sterling Ethos, 2017)

The Good Witch's Perpetual Planner
(cowritten with Shawn Robbins, Sterling Ethos, 2019)

The Wiccapedia Spell Deck:
A Compendium of 100 Spells &
Rituals for the Modern-Day Witch
(cowritten with Leanna Greenaway
and Shawn Robbins, Sterling Ethos, 2020)

The Modern-Day Witch 2023
Wheel of the Year 17-Month Planner
(cowritten with Shawn Robbins, Sterling Ethos, 2022)

Dedication

This book is dedicated to the many teachers I have had over the years. All of the teachers I have had have given me different insights and approaches to magic. Without each of you, I would not be the witch I am today.

First off, to Valerie Walker, who is known in the Feri Tradition as Veedub. She encouraged me to find ways to keep my practice going even when I didn't feel like I had energy for anything. She explained that by trying to do some work, my practice can actually energize me and revitalize my spirit. Thanks to her advice, I tried a few of the Feri techniques, and they have now become a part of my daily practice.

Secondly, I would like to dedicate this book to Christopher Penczak. My heart has been with the Temple Tradition since I first met him in 2008 during a Witchcraft III weekend intensive course. He encouraged me to just give a technique a try a few times before removing the concept from my practice. This encouragement helped me have a deeper appreciation for those who follow very ritualized and formalized magical practices.

Thirdly, I dedicate this book to Mama Starr Casas, who taught me Conjure. From her I learned how to read folktales and gather the hidden wisdom. Starr taught me how to read my Bible for magical work hidden within. She taught me the importance of honoring one's ancestors (whom she defined can be any passed loved one you consider family, as well as teachers and respected elders) and keeping the memory of our ancestors alive. Much of what I learned from Starr I have applied to other areas of my life with great reward.

Finally, I would like to dedicate this book to the many authors whose books I have read over the years. Each book I read helped me develop my eclectic path. Scott Cunningham, Raymond Buckland, Raven Grimassi, and Silver RavenWolf are just a few of the many authors whose books have guided me and helped me become the witch I am today.

CONTENTS

PART III: RESOURCES

Disclaimer

The publisher and author assume no liability for any injuries caused to the reader that may result from the reader's use of content contained in this publication and recommend common sense when contemplating the practices described in the work. In the following pages you will find recommendations for the use of certain essential oils, incense blends, and ritual items. If you are allergic to any items used in the rituals, please refrain from use. Essential oils are potent; use care when handling them. Always dilute essential oils before placing them on your skin, and make sure to do a patch test on your skin before use. There are spells in this text that deal with mental illness support. These spells are to supplement proper treatment for your mental health, and they are not substitutions for treatment by a professional. If you are in crisis, talk to a professional and get proper treatment first. Only use the spells after seeking professional help.

Introduction

A wife sits at home in front of a candle and tears her husband's old shirt. Her husband is a solider and is currently serving across seas. She tears and cuts the shirt into the shape of a human. As she begins to sew up the sides of the shirt, she whispers prayers for protection and strength. She fills the doll with herbs and crystals that have potent magic to protect her loved one. When the doll is full, she sets it on her altar upon the pentacle for protection. She keeps the doll there, holding it daily and praying over it, until her husband comes home from war.

A young couple is given part of the wife's father's land to start their own family. As they build their home, a small pit is dug by their front door. The couple places a jar full of hair, nails, rust, and other sharp objects in the pit and buries the jar, filling in the pit. The young couple now feels comfortable knowing their home will be protected; they have just buried their witches' jar.

A young girl sits in front of a blue candle surrounded by a variety of herbs and crystals. Incense burns as she gently places a selection of each of the herbs and crystals into a small blue drawstring bag. She holds back tears as she places a photo of her sick mother into the bag and fills it with more crystals and herbs. When the bag is full, she holds it to her heart and draws the bag close. She places the charm into her purse and carries it with her everywhere. When she thinks of her mother, she plays with the bag, sending healing to her mother no matter where she is.

Each of the stories above illustrates a different style or type of magic. The wife of the soldier worked a poppet spell to strengthen the protection around her husband, ensuring that he would come home safe from his deployment. The young couple created a witches' jar, which lore states will destroy and tear apart any ill will sent their way. The young girl created a healing charm bag to heal her mother of whatever was ailing her.

In this book you will have a chance to explore a variety of magical techniques involving container magic. You will learn how to use jars, bottles, balls, boxes, sachets, packets, and poppets. You will learn how to make your own witches' jars and money spells. Within this work you will learn how to choose the right container, select the right fillings, and what to do if your spell backfires or does not work. You will learn how to feed and work your containers and how to create your own containers for your spells.

I have been a practicing witch for more than twenty years. I am a primarily self-taught witch with a second-degree initiation into the Temple of Witchcraft tradition. Over my many years of practice, I have studied many different forms of witchcraft and magic. As I explored American folk magic, the practice of Hoodoo, also called Conjure, woke something deep within my spirit.

I took the initiative to seek training in Conjure. While I was searching for a teacher, I read many books and talked to many different practitioners online. One of the books I read was *The Complete Conjure Workbook Volume 1: Working the Root* by Starr Casas. She has since published several other Conjure works that provide traditional material that has not been shared anywhere else.

Starr was one of the authors who not only knew what they were talking about but also lived it daily. She began writing and teaching Conjure to preserve the work. As an elder, she has watched Conjure become sanitized as people have altered traditional practices and replaced animal curios with nontraditional materials. To stop this process, she started her online Conjure Academy to teach Conjure as she was taught and knows it. I enrolled and completed training in the Conjure Academy.

The material in this book comes from both Conjure work and modern witchcraft. Witchcraft and Conjure come from two different cultures. The witchcraft I'm familiar with is mostly based on European folk magic and folklore. Conjure as a magical tradition was created during slavery by enslaved people to survive and preserve what they could of their ancestral heritage.

In this text you will see *Conjure* capitalized to differentiate it from the practice of conjuring (summoning and calling) spirits. Likewise, the word *witchcraft* will all be lowercase to represent the magical practice of witchcraft. A capitalized *Witchcraft* refers to the religion of Witchcraft, which in some cases is known as Wicca.

Conjure work comes from a place of survival. The works that came out of Conjure can involve animal parts, such as hearts, tongues, and livers. Many of the suggested animal parts in this book, such as beef tongue, can be purchased at your local meat market. Parts like alligator teeth and claws can be obtained from Conjure and traditional witchcraft specialty shops. There is no reason to harm any animal to obtain the materials. You either obtain them ethically or not use them at all.

I was taught by Starr that Conjure is open to everyone as long as they remember the roots of the work, honoring those who died as enslaved people preserving their culture. When the enslaved people were freed, they ended up, in most cases, joining poor minority groups. While living in these communities, they shared magical practices that eventually exposed Conjure to non-Black Americans.

Almost every Conjure work will contain a Bible verse or prayer to be used with it. The Bible is a huge part of Conjure. The use of Bible verses was how Conjure work survived and remained hidden for years. You do not need to be Christian to work Conjure. You just need to respect the Bible and view the Bible as a powerful magical tool and book.

In Conjure it is believed that the ability to do magic comes from the Divine. They believe that when it said humanity was created in God's image it included the ability to work magic. For a Conjure worker, any work they do is the work of God. Conjure workers also believe that there is a spirit in everything bestowed by God.

The belief in animism is one of the reasons that Conjure and witchcraft can work well together. Both traditions work with the spirit or forces within the materials to work magic. While they may approach animism differently, this similarity makes cross-cultural communication possible.

Throughout this text the term *curio* will be used to refer to a variety of materials used as fillings in container spells. The term *curio* is used in both Conjure and witchcraft to refer to a variety of materials used in spellwork. Curios are nonherb or nonroot objects and materials used in magical work. The materials can be synthetic or natural. It's the symbolism and energetic properties that matter.

Within this text you will also find hexes and curses. Baneful magic should be a last resort and only used after you have tried everything else to solve your problem. Ask yourself the following questions before working baneful magic. Is this morally and ethically right for you? Can you accept the consequences of your actions? Finally, will you regret inaction?

If the answers are "yes," then do the work. If the answers are "no," don't cast the spell. If you might regret the work, don't cast the spell. If you are not 100 percent certain about the spell and the actions you are about to take, the spell can and will backfire on you.

All of the spells and rituals in this book have been written by me. These spells are adapted from spells that I have personally used and had success with. You will not find these spells anywhere else. Even the traditional Conjure works have been modified slightly by me to suit my magical style.

This book has been divided into three different parts. The first part of the book is all about the basics of container magic. Here you will learn about what container magic is, what the different types of containers can be, how to fill your container, and how to dispose of your containers. Part 2 is all about the practical magical work. The last section of this book is a resource section.

It is my hope that by the end of this book you will not only have an understanding of the different forms of container magic but also an understanding of the different approaches to working your magic. I hope that you will be able to look at the various containers in your life with new light and see that magic can be worked with whatever materials you have on hand.

PART I
THE BASICS

Getting Started
with Container Magic

Magic is the practice of manipulating energy and shaping that energy. One of the most famous definitions of magic comes from Aleister Crowley. He wrote in his book *Magick in Theory and Practice* that "magick is the science and art of causing change to occur in conformity with the Will."[1] In essence, magical work is a way for us to gain power over our lives and create changes for a better life.

There are many ways to practice magic. Candle magic is one of the most popular forms of spellwork. The popularity of candle magic comes from producing quick results. Once the candle has finished burning, all of the energy has been

---

1. Crowley, *Magick in Theory and Practice.*

released. For those who are seeking a long-term magical work with a consistent flow of energy, there is container magic.

All forms of magic use and raise energy. Candle spells and kitchen witchery raise and gather the energy as they build the spell and release it to end the spell. In container magic spells, the energy is released over time. The gradual release of energy makes container magic perfect for long-term goals.

What Is Container Magic?

Container magic is a type of folk magic that comes in many forms, such as charm bags, jar spells, and poppet spells. Any magical work where you fill an object with charged materials and play with it daily to release the magic is a container magic spell. By filling the containers with magical correspondences, you have created a charm that represents the change you want to have in your life. Container magic takes containers used for storage and turns them into powerful magical tools.

In modern witchcraft, mojo bags or charm bags are most commonly used as container magic. For Conjure workers, jar and bottle spells are the most well-known form of container magic. It is not uncommon to see the terms *witches' jar* or *witches' bottle* used interchangeably. While they are different containers, any magical work you do in a jar can be done in a bottle. Bottles can be easier to travel with, making them an excellent choice for charms that will be carried with you.

Poppet spells are ideal spells for targeting specific individuals. These containers are human-shaped or animal-shaped "dolls." Whatever happens to the doll should happen to its target. These spells are a form of sympathetic magic.

With small exceptions, most packets are small containers that are carried with you every day until your goal manifests. The packets are stuffed with herbs and curios that align with the desired manifestation. Sachets, charm bags, and mojo bags are small drawstring bags that are carried with you. The terms *sachet* and *charm bag* are interchangeable. Mojo bags are a specific form of Conjure charm bag.

How Container Magic Works

A fundamental magical philosophy is that everything has energy. Energy in magical work exists on a subtle frequency that can only be experienced through psychic or spiritual means. When we work magic, we take these energies and program them with intent or desire.

For example, candle magic has two sources of energy. The first is the physical burning of the candle. Our mental focus is the other energy source. As the candle burns, both sources of energy are released.

Container magic is a little different. Every material used as a filling for your container provides energy for the work at hand. As the materials are gathered and worked into the container, the energy grows and changes shape. It is the focusing

13

of our intent into the container that connects the various energetic forms and creates a new cohesive whole.

Container magic is a two-stage process. The first part involves the selection of materials and physical creation of the container. In some cases, the container will be created as part of the spell process. The second part is the sealing and final boost. This is where the use of incense, oils, and candles begins. Each additional material provides some release for the spell. The spell can then draw on the energy stored within the container as needed until the work manifests.

When we cast a spell, we create an energetic packet or thought form that gets sent into the universe to manifest our goal. With candle magic and kitchen witchery, that thought form is created from your intent and is released when the spell is released. These thought forms have only have an origin source of energy, while the thought forms created through container magic have multiple sources of energy.

The thought forms created are living spirits that need to be nourished. Feeding the spirit is as simple as anointing the container with a related oil or passing the container through incense again. The energy from the incense or oil feeds the spirit, allowing them to continue their work. As long as the entity is fed, the spell will work.

Container Seals

One reason why container magic works well for long-term goals is that you can seal containers. Sealing a container preserves the magic within the container. The stored energy within the sealed container is only released when being worked or when the seal is broken by you. This is why when a container breaks, the spell must be recreated; the energy was released before the final manifestation.

When sealing your container, consider if you are going to use the container again or not. Any container that you intend to repurpose needs to have a seal that comes undone readily. Witches' jars are containers that require permanent seals.

Jars and bottles are sealed through their caps or lids. Sachets are kept shut through a drawstring. Packets are sealed through stitches or other such methods. Poppets are sealed based on the materials they are made from.

Choosing Your Container

When choosing a container for your magic, the first thing to consider is what the goal of the work is and if that goal targets a single person or a large area. For a magical goal that is focused on a large area or multiple people, a stationary container, such as a jar or box, would be the best choice. Being placed in a stationary position allows these charms to work their magic most effectively. When the work targets a single person, poppets, sachets, and packets are ideal containers to use. Of course, you also want to make sure you can fit all of your fillings into the container.

Once you have your goal in mind, ask yourself how you are going to try and reach that goal. When you are casting the spell and doing the magical work, you want to be sure that the materials used for the container will be able to with-stand the actions taken in the spell (burning, stabbing, freez-ing, burying, etc.). The exception is if you want the container destroyed as part of the spell.

How long term is this goal? Jars, boxes, and balls are ideal for semipermanent magical works. These containers are designed for long-term use. Sachets and charm bags are designed to be easily filled and emptied. Their openings make them ideal for short-term goals or goals that adapt and change with time. Packets and poppets are better for goals that can be either short term or long term as they can be made out of materials that are durable and able to be used for more than one spell, or they can be made out of materials that are dis-posable with the spell.

Last, do you plan on using the container again in other works? Some of the containers can be used for multiple mag-ical works. Jars, bottles, and boxes are all containers that can be used again. If you plan on disposing of the container as part of the work or after the work is done, then choose a disposable container.

Since container magic is meant to be practical, use mate-rials that you have on hand or can easily obtain. Remember, each container has its strengths and weaknesses. Depending on the work at hand, some containers may be better suited to the goal than others. Many of the containers used in con-tainer magic can be found around your house or at a local flea market.

Jars are easy to obtain. Many food items come processed in jars at the grocery store. You can also find unused jars in the canning goods section of garden or hardware stores. Boxes are also readily available. Most items are shipped in some sort of box, making them easy to obtain. Poppets can be easily made or purchased anywhere dolls are sold. Containers can be found nearly everywhere in a variety of shapes and sizes.

Cleansing & Cleaning Your Containers Before Use

Before containers can be used magically, they must be cleansed. Cleaning the containers removes physical and energetic residue. The only energy you want is energy that you put there.

SOAP & WATER CLEANSE

Use this ritual to cleanse any containers that are safe to get wet.

MATERIALS
- Wash basin, kitchen sink, or tub
- Hot water
- For plastic, glass, and metal containers: 1 teaspoon dish soap
- For fabric containers: 1 teaspoon laundry soap
- Fresh, clean sponge
- 1 teaspoon lemon juice or lemon essential oil (to clear away and cut past energy)
- ¼ teaspoon vinegar (to remove past energy)

WORKING

1. Fill the basin, sink, or tub with hot water. Add the appropriate soap.

2. Add the lemon juice and the vinegar. Stir the mixture with the sponge until well mixed.

3. Wash the container until all residue is removed. As you clean the container, chant:

   Cleanse and clean, cleanse and clean.
   I remove the energy that is unseen.

4. Rinse the container with clean water to remove soap residue.

5. Set the container aside to dry. Place in storage when dry.

DRY CONTAINER CLEANSE

Use this ritual to cleanse any container you do not wish to get wet or that would be damaged by water.

The recipe for cleansing incense can be found in the "Incense Recipes" section of part 3. Frankincense or sage stick incense are substitutes.

MATERIALS
- Cleansing incense
- Lighter or matches
- Charcoal disc and censer/incense burner
- Dusting cloth

WORKING

1. Light the incense using the lighter or matches.

2. Pass the container through the incense smoke five to seven times chanting:

   Cleanse and clean, cleanse and clean.
   I remove the energy that is unseen.

3. Wipe down the container with the cloth, removing everything.

4. Extinguish the incense, and place the container in storage until needed.

Container Choice & Availability

Container magic is highly adaptable. Many spells can work in any or multiple types of containers. You can work with what you have on hand rather than buying something.

When two or more containers seem to be appropriate for the work at hand, use divination to find the answer. For this, you will want a tool that can answer your questions with "yes," "no," or "maybe." I personally prefer using pendulums for divination. Pendulums can be made out of almost anything. To make one, you simply need to hang a weight from a chord or string and let it swing freely.

CONTAINER DIVINATION

With your form of divination chosen, use this exercise to decide which container to use.

MATERIALS
- Form of yes/no/maybe divination
- Potential containers for your magic

WORKING
1. Ask the tool what "yes" is.

2. Ask what "no" and "maybe" are.

3. Once the answers are established, hold each container in your hand and ask your tool of choice if it is the container for the spell at hand. Place the containers in "yes," "no," and "maybe" piles.

4. Repeat step 3 with the containers in the "yes" and "maybe" piles until one item remains.

Reuse of Containers

For the best results, keep your containers to one type of work. Over time the containers will develop a base charge and you may find a spirit there. This power can be tapped into as you work with the container.

If you need to change intent between uses, you must cleanse the container. Cleansing removes traces of magical work. Physically cleaning the containers removes both physical and energetic residue.

RETURN TO STORAGE
CLEANSING BATH

This wash is primarily for cleaning between spells. The herbal materials used clear all energy.

MATERIALS
- Wash basin, kitchen sink, or tub
- Hot water
- For plastic, glass, and metal containers: ¼ to ½ teaspoon dish soap
- For fabric containers: ¼ to ½ teaspoon laundry soap
- Fresh, clean sponge
- 1 dried bay leaf
- 4 drops pine essential oil
- 4 drops eucalyptus essential oil
- Container to be washed

WORKING
1. Fill the basin, sink, or tub with hot water. Add the appropriate soap.

2. Add the remaining materials. Swirl the water with the sponge until well mixed.

3. Scrub the container, removing all physical residue. As you clean the container, chant:

   Cleanse and clean, remove the energy that is unseen.

4. Place the container where it can dry without being disturbed. Once dry, place it in storage.

CONTAINER FILLINGS

Crucial to container magic are the fillings. For effective magic, choose your materials carefully. A container put together haphazardly will not work. The more attention you give to the container, the more effective your spell will be. Each material you fill your container with needs to correspond to the work at hand. Many herbs and curios have similar general correspondences. By looking at the subtle differences, you can choose the best materials.

Petitions

Your containers should include a petition. Petitions are written statements of intent. The petitions should include specific details while being as general as possible. Petitions should be written as if the goal had manifested in that moment. This both tells and shows the forces involved what the desired outcome is.

Do not be *too* general with your petitions. If you just write your petition simply stating: "I wish to be employed," you could end up with a job you hate. The spell worked. You found a job; it just wasn't what you actually wanted. To prevent landing an unwanted job, the petition should be rewritten with more general specifics. The new petition might look like: "I (your name) wish to have a job working in (desired field). In this job I am able to apply and use (list the job skills). I have (state the benefits you need). My boss is (list what you are looking for in a boss), and my coworkers are (talk about the team you want to be a part of). My pay is (insert pay rate) and my commute is (talk about the commute you want to have)."

Once you are satisfied with how you have worded the petition, it is time to write the final copy. The final copy must be perfect with no mistakes of any kind, so be careful and pay close attention to the details. Date and sign your final petition. The final copy might look something like this:

Date: _____

Petition: _____

_____

_____

_____

Signature: _____

WRITE A PETITION

A well-written petition burned over a candle is a spell all on its own. The following exercise guides you through the process of creating and writing your own petition with the option to burn it. Use the exercise to practice this simple form of magic.

MATERIALS
- Pen
- 2 pieces of paper
- Candle, optional
- Matches or lighter, optional
- Firesafe container, optional

EXERCISE
1. On one piece of paper, use the pen to write down your general goal. Under the goal, write out important specific details related to it. Start writing draft sentences of your petition. Read each draft aloud before continuing.

2. When you have chosen which petition draft to use, write a copy on the second piece of paper. The clean copy is the one you will use in your spell.

3. If you wish to burn your petition, light the candle with the matches or lighter.

4. Hold your petition over the candle, and read it aloud with confidence.

5. After you have read the petition, use the candle's flame to light the petition on fire. Carefully put the burning petition in the firesafe container, and let the candle burn out completely.

Sigils

Sigils are a powerful source of magic, and it is easy to create your own. Everything you need to create a sigil can be found in your petitions. To create your own sigil, follow the steps of writing a petition. Once you have the final copy of your petition, cross out all of the repeated letters. Make a list of the remaining letters, and create a design using those letters and any flourishes or design elements that appeal to you. When you have decided on your completed design, redraw the design—your sigil—on a clean piece of paper, being careful to avoid any mistakes. This is one method of sigil creation, and I have the most experience with this specific method.

CREATE A SIGIL

This sigil magic starts with a simple petition. This exercise will take you through one way to work and craft sigils. Use it to practice sigil magic for yourself. After you give it a try, research the many other ways to create and use sigils in magic.

MATERIALS
- Pen
- 2 pieces of paper

EXERCISE

1. Using the pen, write out your final petition on a piece of paper. Make sure to include all important details related to the intent at hand.

2. Cross out all duplicate letters. Review your petition, ensuring you got every letter.

3. Still working on the same piece of paper, make a list of the remaining letters. If there are no remaining letters, reword your petition so that there will be leftover letters.

4. Create a design where all the remaining letters are intertwined and integrated together. Add any flourishes and decorations you would like to make the design attractive.

5. Once you have your final design, take the clean piece of paper and redraw your sigil cleanly. It is now ready to be used in your magic.

Personal Effects

Any containers that target specific individuals should include a personal effect. Personal effects are things like hair, nails, body fluids, and used clothes. Alternatives to personal effects are taglocks. A taglock is another item connecting to your target. Taglocks can be photos or drawn images or business cards. Both personal effects and taglocks tap into and work with the target's energy.

Working magic for other people is very tempting, but before you work magic for another person, you need to have their consent. Casting a spell without their consent is imposing your will and interfering with their free will. There are exceptions to interfering with free will.

The first exception is baneful magic, which is used to force a change in behavior. Generally speaking, you don't want the target of curses or hexes to know they've been targeted. Sweetening spells are the second exception. A sweetening spell is about subtle influences rather than direct control.

Dirt, Herbs, Crystals & Animal Parts

After petitions and personal effects, the next items to put in your container would be dirt, herbs, roots, crystals, and curios. These ingredients must always correspond to your intent. Part 3 contains lists that will help you choose these elements.

Dirt

Dirt contains the essence of the genius loci, or the spirit of a place. When you are working with dirt, you have a material that will contain the essence of everything related to or within the location you sourced it. Dirt has highly concentrated energy, so not much is needed in spells.

With dirt containing the essence of the land spirit, it is important to give an offering to the spirit before and after you gather the dirt. Giving an offering shows respect for that spirit. Some offerings include water, coins, food, and your hair.

You can also use dirt that plants grew in. Using the dirt that plants grew in is a great way to use herbal energies even when the plant has long died. To gather this dirt, simply sweep up a handful of dirt from the plant when you harvest. Remember to store the plant and dirt separately.

It is easy to gather dirt for magical use, even when in public. To gather dirt all you need is to carry some plastic bags and tissues in your pockets. Gathering dirt is as simple as bending over, scooping up a few grains with tissues, placing them in the bag, and walking away. You can put the dirt in better storage when you get home. Remember that gathering dirt from private property can be considered trespassing. Use your discretion. If it does not feel right to take the dirt, don't.

GATHERING DIRT WITH ESSENCE OF THE LAND SPIRIT

Use this technique to start gathering and working with dirt in your magical practice.

MATERIALS
- Tissues
- Offering for spirit, such as coins, water, food, hair, etc.
- Small plastic bags
- Containers
- Permanent marker

EXERCISE

1. Choose a location that relates to a current magical goal.

2. The next time you are at the location, prepare to gather some dirt for your work.

3. Ask permission from the spirit and give an offering.

4. If the spirit doesn't give permission, come back another time.

5. If the spirit does give permission, gather the dirt by scooping some up with the tissues and placing it in the bags. Give a second offering.

6. Once you've gathered what dirt you can and made the second offering, return home. Store the dirt in containers labeled with permanent marker.

Herbs and Roots

Herbs and roots are often used as fillings for containers. When choosing your herbs and roots, you want to have something to attract your goal, something to help with your luck, and something to protect what you are trying to obtain. One of the herbs or roots chosen will be the primary source of energetic power in the work. This is the herb or root you will have the most of. Fresh herbs and roots are the best, as they still contain life energy. Dried herbs and roots work; it just takes more for the same effect. See part 3 for herbal and root correspondences.

Crystals

Crystals can be used in any form of container magic. When working with crystals, it is important to consider the other materials that will be used in the container. There are some crystals that become toxic or damaged when they interact with water. If you are unsure about your crystal, work with caution and do not involve liquids. The crystal resource list in part 3 includes correspondences, and there is an asterisk next to those that should never be used with water.

Animal Parts

Finally, another common item that you may find in container works are animal parts. The parts used are obtained through finding them in nature or buying them from ethical specialty shops. Some items, such as cat whiskers and claws, shed naturally; others do not. No matter, no animals should be harmed gatherings these materials. Only use animal parts that you can ethically obtain. Again, see the resource section for an expanded curio list.

CHARGING YOUR CONTAINER

Once you have your fillings it's time to build the container and charge it for the work at hand. Filling the containers and charging them is one of the many fun parts of working container magic. Petitions are the first thing placed in any container, as they are full of pure intent, and all of the other materials are used to enhance the power within the petition.

After the petition comes any personal effects used. Personal effects tie the petition to the target. As you add the personal effects, you need to give the effects life. You give personal effects life by exhaling over them and giving them a job. The exhale returns some life force to the effect and the job tells the effect what is expected of it. While exhaling over the effects, state:

(Personal effect), you are (target's name).
All magic here will impact (target's name).

Waking the Spirit & Energy

As other materials are added to the containers, they also need to be woken up and told what to do. When we activate the energy, we are accessing the spiritual force of that material. By activating the energy and the spirit, we are able to manipulate and direct that energy. While it is possible to sense the energy before waking it up, it remains dormant. When we wake the spirit up, the full potential of the energy is available for the job ahead of them.

The following techniques provide different ways to awaken the energy and spirit. You can use the techniques individually or together. Try all of them, and find which technique works best for you. The most important thing is you have a way to tap into that energy and direct it toward the work at hand. I personally use the first and second techniques together in order to provide as much power as possible. I use the third technique the first time I work with a new material.

One of the techniques is based in an animistic view. This technique awakens the spirit directly. Your breath provides the force, which gives fresh life to the spirit. In the technique, you exhale over the material three times. Each breath provides a different level of awareness. The first breath awakens the spirit from rest, the second breath activates the physical materials, and the third breath you provide gives the spirit its job.

Between each breath visualize the energy within becoming stronger and brighter. Each breath should bring out a more intense connection. By the time you are done with the breaths, you should feel the life flowing through and around the material freely. The filling is now ready to be used.

The second technique involves physically tapping the materials. Physical touch draws the attention of the corresponding spirit. Each time the fillings are touched, the energy output gets stronger and easier to manipulate. When the vibrations are steady, the curio is ready to work.

In the third technique, you try to sense the vibrations of each material. By accessing the vibrations of the material, you are able to directly program that energy for magical work. The technique is based on a principle called the law of vibration from *The Kybalion*, which states that "Nothing rests; everything moves; everything vibrates."[2]

WAKE THE SPIRIT

This exercise and technique works best on materials that were once part of something living. In this technique, you provide a new source of life for the material.

---

2. Three Initiates, *The Kybalion*, 13.

MATERIALS
- Filling
- Your breath

EXERCISE

1. Take three slow breaths to bring your attention to the task at hand.

2. Pick up the filling and hold it in your hand. Take a minute to feel the energy as it is now.

3. Inhale. Before you exhale, hold the material and state:

   (Name/type of material), I awaken you from your slumber.

4. Exhale over the material. As you exhale, feel the spirit begin to stir within.

5. Take a second breath. Before you exhale, state:

   (Name/type of material), I give you life this day.

6. Exhale over the material. As you exhale, feel the material show signs of being awake.

7. When you feel that the material is fully awake, it's time for the third and final breath. Inhale. Before you exhale, state:

   (Name/type of material), I ask you today to provide energy my way. I ask of you to (the spirit's job).

8. Exhale over the material, providing life energy to it.

9. Hold the material until you feel it vibrating and pulsating with the programmed energy. Once the material is pulsating at a rate you find acceptable, it's ready to work for you.

TAPPING INTO THE ENERGY

This exercise works best for crystals, dirt, and shells. This technique taps into the essence within these materials.

MATERIALS
- Filling
- Container

EXERCISE

1. Pick up the filling you wish to tap into.

2. Place the material in the palm of your nondominant hand. With the opposite hand, use the middle and index finger to tap three times on the curio, stating:

   I call upon the energy within (material) to be with me this day.

3. Draw and direct the energy from the material to a point in front of you. See the energy begin to flow from the material to that point. As the energy begins to flow, start shaping the energy into a ball.

4. Tap the curio three times more, stating:

   I draw this energy from you to work a spell that's new.

5. Repeat step 3. The energy should feel stronger. Continue to manipulate that energy into a ball.

6. Again, tap the curio three times, stating:

   (Material), to help me achieve my desire, you add (their job). Your help lends fuel to the fire.

7. Draw energy from the curio for the last time. Then take the large energy ball you have created push it back into the material until you see it glow and pulsate. The material is now ready to work.

8. Place the material in the container. Feel the energy flowing from the material to the container. As you add other materials, make sure to notice how the energy mingles, forming an entirely new energetic force by the end of the spell.

VIBRATING IN HARMONY

This exercise can be used for any material. Attuning an item energetically allows for personalized connections and correspondences.

MATERIALS
- Filling
- Container
- Pen
- Paper

EXERCISE

1. Pick up the item and hold it between your hands.

2. Close your eyes and take a breath in. As you exhale, recite the following chant repeatedly:

    I vibrate in harmony with (material).

3. Recite the chant until you and the filling are vibrating as one. When the two vibrations meld into one, you are energetically aligned. As you begin to align with the material, take note of any sensations or images that arise. These sensations and images may be a personal correspondence for you.

4. Tell the material what its job is. Notice the subtle changes in the vibrations as the material sets to its work. Place it in the container and feel the energy of this material melding with any of the other materials.

5. Use the pen to write down what sensations you experienced during this exercise on the sheet of paper. These feelings may provide keys to your personal magical work.

Programming the Container

Between fillings, the container needs to be programmed. Programming the container aligns all the materials with the work at hand. Each ingredient provides a unique energy signature, and programming is how the various energy is molded into one singular force.

One way to program the container is to focus colored light energy surrounding and emanating from the container. If you are unable to visualize colored light, simply focus on the energy. As you focus on the energy, direct images and thoughts of your goal into the energy. This direction of mental energy takes the individual energetic signatures and melds them into one.

Another way to program your container is by physically mixing the materials. The physical mixing or shaking of the container adds another layer of energy. Your physical energy is transferred into the container and transformed into energy for the spell. This energy used to mix the materials not only blends the materials physically but also blends their energy, creating a new energetic form.

In practice, I have found that using both the colored light and shaking techniques together provide the best results. Both techniques work on their own and have provided me with results. I just notice more substantial results when using both methods over one.

The key in both methods is that the energy is being shaped and programmed, and programming the container prevents energetic chaos and provides direction. You have taken the energy and shaped it into a force that will become the thought form behind your spell.

As the container charges, more energy is added until all of the materials are together. By the time all of the material components have been added, a significant amount of energy has been raised. The energy that you raised has become a thought form with one job.

Sealing the container is the next step. When we seal the container, the final shape of the thought form is established, and the energy is done being raised. The last thing we have to do is release the energy to do its work.

Casting the Spell & Releasing the Energy

Depending on your personal style and flavor, this step can be an elaborate ritual involving incantations and invocation, or it can be as simple as focusing on the energy within and releasing some of that energy to the universe. No method is more effective than another. This is all personal preference.

The simpler way is to hold the container close and focus on that same energetic light used when programming the container. Direct that light into the container. When the energy of the light can no longer be seen, it means the container has been charged and is ready to work.

The next method of spellcasting is a bit more elaborate. In these spells, tools like oils, incense, and candles are used. For those who work with a religious paradigm, this is where you would ask your deities or spirits for help. Here is where any Bible verses, chants, or prayers would be recited too.

When oils are used, the containers must be anointed properly. If the goal is to attract something, the containers are anointed from the bottom of the container to the top, which is symbolic of something growing. If the container is to remove something, you must anoint the container from top to bottom, like removing corn husks. Once the container has been anointed, visualize a light flowing from the container. When the light fades, the container is fully charged.

When using incense, the container is passed back and forth through the smoke multiple times. As the container is passed through the incense smoke, visualize light energy flowing from the container to the incense. When you can no longer sense the light energy, the container is fully charged. When the incense is done burning, the thought form is released into the universe. The spell has been cast.

If you use candles as part of the final charging, hold the container a safe distance over the candle flame and pass it back and forth over the flame, reciting any chants, prayers, or Bible verses at the same time. Like with incense, when the candles stop burning, the thought form is released, and the spell has been cast.

No matter the method used, every day the spell is working, the spirit is releasing the energy. In order for the spell to maintain that energetic force in the universe, the spirit needs to be fed and nourished.

Working, Feeding & Recharging Your Container

Some containers don't require feeding, but most need to be worked, fed, or recharged.

Working the Container

Working the container releases a bit of the energy inside. The released energy nourishes the spirit, allowing the spirit to continue their work.

Working the container is as simple as playing with it, and the best practice is to work the container at least once a day. Working the container daily ensures that energy is released daily. The more containers are worked, the more effective they are at manifesting magic. I typically work my jars and sachets twice a day, once right after waking up in the morning and once before going to bed.

Feeding the Container

When you create your container, you are creating an artificial spirit or thought form. This spirit or thought form is created from the combination of all energetic forces used to create it. The container becomes the body or home for the spirit with the energy in the container feeding the spirit.

The feeding of the containers, while based in an animistic philosophy, has a practical application. Each time you feed the container more energy is provided to the spell. This additional energy maintains the work that has already been done and provides fuel to continue working.

Feeding containers is a simple task. To feed your container, simply anoint the container with an appropriate oil or pass the container through an appropriate incense. The act of anointing the container or passing the container through the smoke "feeds" the container. As you feed the container, recite any chants, prayers, or mantras. These chants once again remind the spirit and the container of the work ahead of them. You should feed the container weekly until the spell manifests.

CONTAINER FEEDING RITUAL

This ritual is for after you have created your container. The spirit is doing the work you asked of it, and to continue to exist and work, the spirit must be fed.

MATERIALS
- Incense or oil corresponding to the work being done
- Matches or lighter
- Charcoal disc and censer/incense burner
- Filled container

EXERCISE
1. Use the matches or lighter to light the incense. If not using incense, ready the oil.

2. Pass the container through the incense smoke five to seven times, or anoint the container with the corresponding oil. As you pass the container through the smoke, or anoint the container with the oil, state:

   I feed you, the spirit of my container, that you be nourished and continue to do work for me.

3. As you perform step 2, feel the spirit and force of the container coming back and growing stronger through the energy you are feeding the container.

4. When you feel that the container has been fed enough, extinguish the incense, or put away the oil. Place the container back where you were keeping it.

Recharging the Container

Along with working and feeding your containers, recharging your containers is another part of the process. Some containers are designed to have an indefinite life span. These containers should be recharged once a month. Recharging refreshes the container's energy and provides a fresh boost—almost as if the spell was just cast.

The following ritual requires an altar or workspace. If you maintain a regular altar, you can simply use your working altar. For those who do not have an altar, a large, flat surface is required.

CONTAINER RECHARGING RITUAL

The materials list for this ritual can be adapted to suit your container and the work you have done. For best results, perform this ritual once a month. This ritual can be used as part of any full or new moon esbat ritual.

The candle used in this ritual will be used until the candle is fully burned. Carve a new candle when the first candle has burned out. Anoint the new candle and continue the ritual as written.

When it comes to the crystals, miniature wands or pyramid-shaped clear quartz are best. For best result, the four crystals of your choice should be one type. Two or more crystals can be used for this ritual suitably, but the important thing is that the magic of the crystals correspond to the work being done by the container.

MATERIALS

- 4 clear quartz crystals
- 4 crystals of your choice
- 1 large votive candle with a color that corresponds to the goal or work at hand
- Pin, needle, or knife
- Anointing oil that corresponds to the work
- Candle holder
- Incense with a scent that corresponds to the work
- Charcoal disc and censer/incense burner
- Matches or lighter
- Container to be charged

WORKING

1. Take the four quartz crystals and place them on an altar or workspace in the four cardinal directions. Place the crystals so that the points are directed out and away from the altar. As you place the crystals, be sure to leave plenty of space in the center so that the candle, incense, and container may be placed.

2. Take the four other crystals and place one at each of the cross quarters. Set these crystals facing the same way as the quartz crystals.

3. With your dominant hand, take the pin, knife, or needle and carve one or two words or symbols into the candle. Those words need to be related to the main intent behind the container.

4. Anoint the candle with three to five drops of the anointing oil. Remember to anoint the candle based on if you are attracting or removing something. Put the candle holder in the center of the circle, and place the candle in the candle holder.

5. Place the incense in your burner of choice and place it next to the candle.

6. Using the matches or lighter, light the candle and incense. Make sure that the incense is properly smoking or smoldering before moving onto the next step.

7. Begin recharging the container by anointing the container with the same oil you anointed the candle with. As the container is anointed, make a statement of intent, stating that the oil feeds, powers, and charges the container.

8. Pass the container through the incense smoke, then safely over the candle flame. As you pass the container through the smoke and over the flame, repeat any of the words said during the original creation of the container.

9. After all of the words have been spoken, focus on the container. Hold the container tight in your hands or against your chest. While holding the container tight, focus on feeling and visualize seeing the colored light that surrounded the container when you made it.

10. As you focus and visualize the colored light, begin to shake and manipulate the container. Direct the energy you have raised into the container.

11. When the energy within the container seems like it is ready to burst, set the container back on your altar or work surface. Take your hands and place them over the container. As you hold your hands over the container, direct the bursting energy into the eight crystals on the altar. These crystals will take the energy you have just raised and send it out to the universe.

12. Once you feel that the excess flow of energy has been directed to the universe and the container's glow has faded to a steady heartbeat rhythm, extinguish the candle and incense.

13. Take your dominant hand and with your middle and index fingers, draw a pentacle over the container, sealing in the new energy.

14. Return the container to its home to be worked daily until the work manifests. Repeat this ritual as needed monthly.

Ending Spells &
Content Disposal

When you cast a spell, you send energy out to bring you something you want, need, or desire. Ending the spell returns that energy to the universe and yourself.

The main reason why spells end is that they have worked, and your goals have been obtained. Of course, there are sometimes other reasons why spells end or are ended by the caster. One reason to end a spell is that the spell is thought to not be working. Often this incomplete spell is the result of thinking you made a mistake. Another reason you may want to end a spell is that the spell is not working in a way you wanted. When you work magic, you alter the flow of energy in the universe, and this action occasionally brings about unforeseen consequences. In both cases, the spell needs to be undone.

When spells backfire or go wrong, it is important to not only know why but to know how to dismantle and stop the spell. In container magic, the process is simple and begins by breaking the seal and releasing the energy. Once the energy has been released from the container, the disposal of the contents may begin.

Breaking the Seal

The first step in ending the spell is breaking the seal of the container. In some container spells, when you break the seal, you want to destroy the container. Before you destroy the container, make sure you have no future uses for it.

Opening the container automatically releases the energy within. I like to visualize the energy being released like air from a deflating balloon. As the energy leaves the container, it mixes with the air and is dispersed into the universe. With each bit of energy that gets reabsorbed, any ties to your subconscious are cleared, neutralizing any remaining energetic force from the container.

Content Disposal

Now that you've ended the spell it's time to dispose of the contents within the container. Each of the materials used in container magic needs to be dealt with individually. Some of the materials, such as crystals, bones, or other curios, can be used again in a different magical work after cleansing. Some materials can only be used once and need to be properly disposed of.

First, you will need to dispose of any liquids that were used in the container. These liquids are not safe for human or animal consumption. For honey or other thick or fatty liquids, use a spoon to scoop them out and toss them in the trash. Other liquids can be strained in order to separate out the solids. You can then toss the solids into the trash and flush the remaining liquids down the toilet.

Herbs that are being used as container fillings cannot be used again for magical work. They have released and used their energy through the work they just did. Before you dispose of the herbs, you need to thank them for their help. Herbs can then be buried in the ground and allowed to decompose naturally, returning to the earth. Placing the used herbs in the trash is an option. An alternative is to burn the herbs in a cauldron or fire pit. The ashes of the herbs can then be disposed of. Spreading ashes at a stop sign will stop the spell, and disposing of the ashes at crossroads sends the message that the spell is over in all directions.

When photos are used, they will need to be disposed of. Most photos used in spellwork are no longer suitable for display in a frame or photo album. Burning these photos in a fire pit or firesafe container, such as a cast-iron cauldron, is a suitable way to dispose of them.

Your petitions will need to be disposed of too. One way to dispose of them is to cut them into tiny pieces, and toss them into the trash. The most traditional way to dispose of the petition is to burn the petition in a firesafe container, such as a cast-iron cauldron. You can burn the petition by itself or with any photos that need to be disposed of.

Like herbs, personal effects will also need to be disposed of after the work has been done. Materials like hair and nails need to have their energy cut from the spellwork. If the energy is not cut away, it is possible for the magic to still have an impact on the owner of those personal effects.

Fur, shed skin, claws, and whiskers are curios that need to be disposed of once the work has been done. These three curios have the same sort of energetic ties that personal effects contain. Cutting and clearing the magic ensures that the impacts of the magic will stop.

CLEAR PERSONAL EFFECTS & CURIOS

The spell is used when you need to remove and cut away any energetic ties you no longer want. This spell is used to end magical works and can be used to cut any force from your life.

The length of string in the materials list is an estimate and starting point. You want to make sure that you can wrap the string around the container and have room to spare. Before you cut your length of string, do a test wrap of the string to ensure you have enough.

MATERIALS
- Approximately 2 feet of string
- Container used in the magic
- Scissors
- Personal effects such as hair, nails, and teeth (Photos and scraps of old clothes are good substitutes.)

WORKING
1. Wrap one end of string around the container once and tie a knot.

2. Place the string on a working surface and pull the remaining string out so the knot around the container tightens.

3. Place the personal effects at the long end of the string, across from the container.

4. Wrap the string around the personal effects three times, then tie a knot.

5. Pull the container away from the personal effects until the string is as tight as it is going to get.

6. Take the scissors and cut the string. As you cut the string, state:

   I cut the ties that bind. The energy has been released. It's time for the magic work to cease.

7. Untie the personal effects and the container. Toss the personal effects into the trash.

Reusable Contents

There are some fillings that can be used in multiple magical works. Crystals, shells, and bones are some of these contents. These materials usually remain intact and unharmed throughout the spell. By remaining intact, these materials can be reused.

To be reused, these materials must be cleansed and left to recharge their energy for a bit. The most effective method to neutralize the energy is to bury the item in the earth for 12 to 24 hours. The salt burial is an alternative to burying within the earth. Both salt and the earth neutralize energy, allowing it to be transformed into something else.

CLEANSING SALT BURIAL

Salt absorbs and neutralizes the energy it comes into contact with, and this is why you will want to encase the items with salt, if possible. Depending on the size of the items involved and your bowl, it can be possible to cleanse more than one item at a time. When it is not possible to bury more than one item in the bowl of salt, you can bury the items for only an hour at a time. Ideally, the material being cleansed will be buried in the bowl for 12 to 24 hours, but the most important part of this cleansing process is that the material is as completely covered as possible by the salt. Sea salt works best for this ritual, but table salt works just as well.

MATERIALS
- 1 to 2 cups sea salt
- Large bowl
- Item(s) to be cleansed

WORKING
1. Pour the salt into the bowl.

2. With your hands, dig a well or hole in the salt. Once the well or hole has been dug, place the item into it.

3. Cover the item with the salt.

4. Hold your hands over the bowl and visualize the salt drawing out the charge from the item. Hold this visualization for as long as possible. When you can no longer hold the visualization, withdraw your hands and ground as necessary.

5. Place the bowl of salt on your altar—or a location where the bowl will not be disturbed—for the next 12 to 24 hours.

6. After the 12 to 24 hours, dig the item out of the salt and dust it off with your hands. The item can now be placed back into storage for any future use.

After this ritual, the salt can either be disposed of or neutralized and used again. To neutralize the salt, pour it into a clear container. During the next full moon, place the container somewhere in the light of the moon. The moonlight will neutralize any energy that the salt absorbed, returning the salt to a neutral energetic state.

Sunlight and moonlight are two other options to neutralize and recharge crystals and curios for magical work. Both the light of the sun and moon are pure sources of light energy, and any of the above methods will work for neutralizing energy. You just need to direct the energy yourself through words or actions.

PART II
Spells & Magical Works

JAR SPELLS

Jar spells are the quintessential form of container magic as they are some of the easiest containers to find. Jars have been around since humanity learned how to preserve food and drink. Once that happened, humanity needed to create some sort of container to hold the preserved materials in. It would only make sense that people would find magical uses for these new containers.

Today jar spells are among the most common form of container magic encountered. Social media and networking websites are full of photos and spells dealing with various jar spells, and jars provide an easy material to work with in many areas of life, including magic.

In this section, I will cover a variety of jar spells that come from my practice. Each of these spells have been adapted from my personal spell book to be shared with you here.

Traditional European Witches' Jar

When it comes to jar spells, there is nothing more famous than the witches' jar. The traditional witches' jar's primary purpose was to trap and destroy any evil spirits and intent sent to the individual who made the jar. Traditionally this jar is made and then buried under the witch's front porch or doorstep. The jar is kept there until the family moves. When moving to a new house, the old witches' jar is destroyed and a new jar made for the new residence.

A traditional European witches' jar was not (and is still not) a pleasant thing to make. The process of making the jar often involves gathering urine as well as animal dung, rusted nails, and rotten foods. Personal effects are added to the jar as decoys. These items take attacks instead of you. Urine is used as a personal effect and to neutralize evil or negativity. Rusted nails and needles are included to damage the spirits. Mirror and glass fragments are used to cut the evil and reflect the evil back to the sender.

EUROPEAN WITCHES' JAR

This jar spell is a work to protect the home from evil. There must be a personal effect for each family member, and a new jar needs to be created anytime you move to a new home. Because this jar uses urine as an ingredient for magical work, you must be careful. For sanitation and safety, wear gloves when gathering and adding urine. Liquid ammonia, which is found in the cleaning supply sections of many grocery stores, can be a substitute. Wear gloves when handling ammonia.

MATERIALS
- Glass jar with a secure lid
- Personal effects such as hair, nails, and teeth (Photos and scraps of old clothes are good substitutes.)
- Rusty nails (You will need 1 nail per person in the home.)
- 2 or 3 pieces of glass
- 3 to 5 mirror fragments
- 5 pins or needles
- Urine or liquid ammonia

WORKING
1. Place the personal effects into the jar. As you add the personal effects, state:

   To protect (their name), you are (their name), and will take all damage for (their name).

2. Add the rusty nails, glass, mirror fragments, and pins or needles to the jar. As you add these materials to the jar, state:

   To destroy and send back all that is sent as an attack.

3. Add the urine or liquid ammonia to the jar. Cover as much of the material with the liquid as you can.

4. Seal the jar as tightly as you can.

5. Vigorously shake the jar to mix the materials, knowing that any evil or negativity sent your way will be trapped in the jar.

6. Bury the witches' jar under your front porch, or hide it somewhere near your front entrance.

7. When you move to a new home, dig up or remove the witches' jar, and carefully smash the jar. Any evil that was trapped into the jar is now destroyed. Using caution, clean up the remnants of the jar and toss them into the trash.

Conjure Witches' Jars

A Conjure witches' jar is designed to trap and confuse evil. Conjure jars contain seeds, salt, or beads as well as knotted string or wire. It is believed that any evil trapped within the jar remains there until every seed, bead, or salt grain is counted and all of the knots are untied. Mirrors and cut glass reflect these materials back to the spirit, causing confusion and hopelessness.

CONJURE WITCHES' JAR

This jar spell is a work to protect the home from evil. With this jar being meant to protect the home, it is essential that the jar contain a personal effect for each member of the household. A new witches' jar needs to be created anytime you move to a new home. Like a traditional European witches' jar, this jar uses urine in the spell. For sanitation and safety, wear gloves when gathering and adding the urine to the jar. Liquid ammonia works as a substitute. Wear gloves when handling ammonia.

MATERIALS
- Glass jar with a secure lid
- Personal effects such as hair, nails, and teeth (Photos and scraps of old clothes are good substitutes.)
- 1 foot of black thread (Thin wire is a good substitute.)
- 1 to 3 packets of old or dead seeds (Two cups salt or 1 to 3 packets of seed beads work as alternatives.)
- 3 to 5 mirror fragments
- 9 pins or needles
- Urine or liquid ammonia

WORKING
1. Place the personal effects into the jar. As you place each personal effect in the jar, give a breath to each concern and name that personal effect for the person they represent using the following words:

(Personal effect) you are (their name).
I give you life that you may act as a decoy
for (their name). All harm directed at
(their name) will hit you instead.

2. Take the black thread and tie several knots over
   its length. Try to make at least a dozen small
   knots and three larger knots. As you tie each
   knot, state:

   For the evil to pass through, each knot
   must be undone; the string restored to new.

3. Once you have tied several knots in the thread,
   place it into the jar.

4. Pour the seeds into the jar. As you pour the seeds
   into the jar, state:

   To be freed, evil must count all of the seeds.

5. Place the mirror fragments into the jar. As you
   place them, state:

   Mirrors confuse and reflect all that is sent
   as an attack.

6. Add the pins or needles to the jar. As you add the
   pins or needles to the jar, state:

   Pins and needles holding tight, traps the
   negativity, unable to take flight.

7. Add the urine or liquid ammonia to the jar.
   Cover as much of the material as you can.

8. Seal the jar shut.

9. Once the jar is sealed, begin to shake the jar. As you shake the jar, recite the 23rd psalm:

> *The Lord is my shepherd; I shall not want.*
>
> *He makes me to lie down in green pastures;*
>
>> *He leads me beside the still waters.*
>
> *He restores my soul;*
>
>> *He leads me in the paths of righteousness*
>>
>> *For His name's sake.*
>
> *Yea, though I walk through the valley of the shadow of death,*
>
>> *I will fear no evil;*
>>
>> *For You are with me;*
>>
>> *Your rod and Your staff, they comfort me.*
>
> *You prepare a table before me in the presence of my enemies;*
>
>> *You anoint my head with oil;*
>>
>> *My cup runs over.*
>
> *Surely goodness and mercy shall follow me All the days of my life;*
>
>> *And I will dwell within the house of the Lord*
>>
>> *Forever.*

10. Bury the witches' jar under your front porch, or hide it somewhere near your front entrance. When you move to a new home, dig up the witches' jar, and safely smash the jar. Any evil that was trapped into the jar is now destroyed. Using caution, clean up the remnants of the jar and toss them into the trash.

Sweetening Jars

Sweetening magic works in two ways. The first is working to influence someone in some way. This influence can be romantic or sexual, or it can deal with professional situations. The idea is that you want them to be open to you and your existence. The second use of sweetening magic applies the concept that people are attracted to sweet things, thus sugar can be used to draw things to you.

OPEN YOUR BOSS/MANAGER'S MIND

This spell is to be used when your supervisor will not listen to you. Use this spell to open their mind to your suggestions.

MATERIALS
- Glass jar with a secure lid
- Manager or boss's business card or a slip of paper with their name and position (symbolizes your target)
- Approximately 1 cup sugar, divided (to sweeten them)
- 1 dried bay leaf (for intent, wishes)
- Pen
- 1 tablespoon dried rosemary (to open the mind)
- 1 tablespoon dried lavender (to relax the mind and spirit)

WORKING

1. On the back of your target's business card or the slip of paper, write down their date of birth if you know it. If that information is unknown, write down how you know your target.

2. Place the business card or slip of paper into the jar, then sprinkle in a little sugar. As you sprinkle the sugar, state:

   Like sugar is sweet, listen to me when next we meet.

3. Gently shake the jar a little bit, visualizing your target opening up to your suggestions and listening to you.

4. Use the pen to write "Listens to me." or "Takes me seriously." on the bay leaf.

5. Place the bay leaf into the jar, sprinkle in more sugar, and once again give the jar a gentle shake.

6. Next, add the rosemary and lavender to the jar to open the mind and spirit. As you add the herbs, state:

   A closed mind is no find. Herbs of the mind open the path divine.

7. Add the rest of the sugar to the jar.

8. Seal the jar and begin to shake the jar. As you shake the jar, state:

   Boss of mine, open your mind. Hear what I have to say. Open the doors to come what may.

9. As you shake the jar, chant this spell's rhyme and visualize everyone listening to what you have to say and discussions beginning that day to fix the problems.

10. Place the jar on a shelf at home. To keep the jar going, shake the jar twice a day (once in the morning and once at night), reciting the same chant from step 8. Feed and recharge as needed.

11. Once your target has started to listen to you and take your thoughts into consideration you can dispose of the materials inside the jar.

RECONCILIATION SWEETENING SPELL

This spell is to be used when two or more parties have been having a fight. This spell is about making up, hearing each other, and finding a compromise to whatever problem the party was fighting about.

MATERIALS
- Glass jar with a secure lid
- Pen
- Paper
- 2 photographs of the party in a happy and healthy space together
- Rubber band
- ½ cup sugar (for attraction, sweetness)
- 1 tablespoon dried lavender flowers (for love, sweetening)

- 2 tablespoons dried rosemary (for family relationships, an open the mind)
- 1 tablespoon dried red rose petals (for love, passion, romance)
- 1 sodalite tumble (for communication)

WORKING

1. Flip the photos over. On the back of each photo, use the pen to write the names of the people in the photo. Under the names write: "A happy, healthy relationship with understanding and communication."

2. Place one of the photos in the jar.

3. Use the rubber band to bind the second photo to the jar. Have the photo facing out with the back against the jar.

4. Pour the sugar into the jar. As you add the sugar, state:

   Like sugar is sweet, in the middle do both sides meet.

5. Sprinkle the lavender flowers around the photo in the jar. State:

   Lavender for love and emotional strength. Lavender to bring peace.

6. Sprinkle the rosemary leaves around the photo in the jar. State:

   Rosemary for our relationship and for an open mind.

7. Add the rose petals to the jar. State:

> *Red rose petals for love, romance, and our relationship.*

8. Gently place the sodalite tumble into the jar. As you add it, state:

> *Sodalite for ease of communication and understanding.*

9. Seal the jar. Hold the jar over your heart while you shake it vigorously. As you shake the jar, recite the following chant five to seven times, or until you feel the jar is fully charged. Chant:

> *Strong emotions sweetened today. Hear what I have to say. Together we will solve the problem without delay.*

10. When you feel that the jar is charged and that you have directed all the energy you can into the jar, place it on a shelf in your bedroom where it will not be disturbed and will be hidden from plain view.

11. For the next week, work the jar twice a day, reciting the chant from step 9 three to five times. Continue to work the jar until the situation is resolved and a compromise has been reached.

12. Once the problem has been resolved and both parties have accepted and agreed to the solution, dispose of the contents of the jar with a thank you.

NOTICE MY DESIRE JAR

This jar spell is to be used when you desire a sexual relationship with someone that you know. Only try using this spell if there is a chance that the person is already looking at you in this way. Do not use this spell if you or the target is already involved in a healthy relationship.

MATERIALS
- Glass jar with a secure lid
- Red candle
- Pin, needle, or knife
- Photo of yourself
- Pen
- Photo of your target
- Rubber band
- 1 cup sugar (for attraction)
- Sprig of fresh rosemary (for memory, an open mind)
- 1 tablespoon dried masterwort (to dominate attention)
- 1 tablespoon ground cinnamon (for love, sexuality)
- 1 tablespoon dried damiana leaves (for passion, sexuality)
- 2 tablespoons dried red rose petals (for love, passion)
- Matches or lighter

WORKING
1. Place the jar on your work surface. Using the pin, needle, or knife, carve your target's name into the candle, and place the candle next to the jar.

2. On the back of your photograph, write out your name and date of birth. Under that information, write out your petition that your target desires you sexually or romantically. On the back of your target's photo, write the same petition.

3. Take the rubber band and bind the photos back-to-back. As you bind the photos, state:

   (Insert target's name here) and I are bound. Our passion and desires know no bounds.

4. Place the photographs into the jar, then cover the photos with the sugar. As you pour the sugar, state:

   With sugar this sweet, our two desires do meet.

5. Place the sprig of rosemary into the jar. State:

   Rosemary, herb divine, open (target's name)'s mind to the passion that is mine.

6. Add the masterwort to the jar. As you add the herb to the jar state:

   To attract (target's name)'s gaze and bring a passionate, sexual daze.

7. Sprinkle the cinnamon into the jar. As you sprinkle it, state:

   To increase passion's fire, cinnamon lights the fire.

8. Pour the damiana leaves into the jar. State:

   Damiana leaf, see my desire; open passion's fire.

9. Add the rose petals into the jar. As you add them, state:

   Roses of passion tonight, let our desires take flight.

10. Use the matches or lighter to light the candle. State:

    By candle fire, notice my desire.

11. Seal and shake the jar. As you shake the jar, visualize your sexual needs and desires being met. Direct all of this energy into the jar. When you can no longer hold onto the visualizations, stop shaking the jar, extinguish the candle, and place the jar in your underwear drawer.

12. Light the same candle, and recite the same statement from step 10 daily as you work the jar in the morning before starting your day and in the evening before going to bed. If the candle burns out before the jar's work is complete, get a fresh red candle, and carve it as instructed in step 1. Continue to burn the candle and work the jar until the spell manifests. Dispose of the jar as you see fit.

Money Jars

Money jars, or money pots, are very common spells to find. The simplest money jar is like a child's bank, which collects money until the bank is emptied and the money is spent or put into a real bank.

CLASSIC MONEY JAR

This spell is the most basic money jar spell. In some practices, it is taught that the money in the jar should be donated to local charities to spread the financial blessings and not spent or used for personal means. I will leave it up to you to decide what you want to do.

MATERIALS
- 12-ounce glass jar with a secure lid
- Found money (coins and bills)

WORKING
1. Collect any and all random currency you find around the house or come into contact with during your daily routine. Add this found money to your jar.

2. Once you've added all the money, tighten the jar's lid, then shake the jar enthusiastically. As you shake the jar, see yourself with an abundance of money. While shaking your jar, chant:

   Money flowing free, I have prosperity.

3. Direct all of the energy from your visualizing, physical shaking, and chanting into the jar. Once all of the energy is directed into the jar, place the jar on a shelf where it won't be disturbed.

4. Every morning, shake the jar, and recite the chant three to five times. At the end of the day, remove the lid to the container and add any

money you found that day. Again, tighten the jar's lid, and shake the container, reciting the same chant three to five times.

5. When the jar is full, take all but a handful of coins and deposit the money into savings or donate it to a charity you are fond of.

6. Start this process again with the coins you left behind. Continue this work as long as you want. If you miss a day or two, that's fine; the spell will still be working. The spell only stops working after two or more weeks of not working the jar.

HONEY MONEY JAR

This jar spell uses the sweetness of honey to attract financial stability and prosperity.

MATERIALS
- Small glass jar with a secure lid
- 3 to 5 silver dollars or similarly valued coins
- 1 vanilla bean (for money)
- 1 tablespoon ground cinnamon (for money)
- ¼ cup honey (for attraction, sweetness)

WORKING
1. Start by adding the coins to the jar.

2. Place the vanilla bean in the jar and state:

Vanilla bean opens the way to bring money on this day.

3. Sprinkle the cinnamon around the vanilla bean. As you sprinkle the cinnamon, state:

   Cinnamon spice, bring prosperity that's nice.

4. Add as much honey as you feel is needed. You do not need to fill the jar; just covering the contents will be enough.

5. Seal the jar. Shake it vigorously. As you shake the jar, see yourself surrounded by more money and in a better state of financial stability. While you are shaking the jar, recite the following chant five to seven times:

   Honey money, honey money, sweet prosperity; honey money, honey money, sweet prosperity.

6. Once the jar is fully charged, place the container on a shelf where the jar will not be disturbed and where you have access to the jar.

7. For the next several weeks, shake the jar twice daily, reciting the honey money chant five to seven times until you start to notice the increase in financial prosperity and success. When your goal has manifested, dispose of the materials.

ATTRACT CUSTOMERS & SALES MONEY JAR

This container is used to attract and increase customers at your business. The funds created in this jar should be used on advertising or gifts to further attract new and loyal customers.

MATERIALS

- Glass jar with a secure lid
- Your business card
- 3 silver dollar coins
- Pen
- 4 pieces of paper
- Tape
- Dirt from your business property
- 2 tablespoons dried pine needles (for eternal financial prosperity and recurring prosperity)
- 3 tablespoons ground cinnamon (for money, prosperity)
- 2 tablespoons dried marigold flowers (to protect money)
- 2 tablespoons dried cinquefoil (for fast cash and to attract customers)
- 3 magnets (for attraction)

WORKING

1. Place your business card into the jar, and add the silver dollar coins on top of it.

2. Follow the instructions, found in part 1, on writing a petition, using the paper and pen. Fold the perfected petition in half toward you and put it in the jar.

3. Using the pen and a new piece of paper, follow the instructions, also found in part 1, to create a sigil. Include your business's logo as part of your sigil design. Redraw this sigil design on the fourth piece of paper. Tape the clean sigil to the jar lid with the sigil facing out.

4. Sprinkle the dirt over the business card, coins, and petition.

5. Sprinkle the dried pine needles into the jar. As you sprinkle them, state:

   Pine evergreen tree, brings everlasting prosperity.

6. Add the ground cinnamon. As you add it, state:

   Cinnamon spice, attract sales that are nice.

7. Add the dried marigold flowers, stating:

   Marigold's flowers bright protects our money every night.

8. Sprinkle the cinquefoil into the jar. State:

   Cinquefoil attracts customers fast, making relationships that last.

9. Place the three magnets into the jar. As you place them, state:

   Magnets to attract customers that keep coming back.

10. Seal the jar, and begin to shake the jar. As you shake the jar, recite this chant five to seven times:

    New customers today; reliable customers that stay.

11. Bring the jar to your work or workspace, and place it somewhere hidden that you can easily access. Whenever you are cleaning, pick up any coins or money you find and add it to the jar. When you do, shake the jar and recite the chant from step 10 five to seven times.

12. At the end of each day, before you go home, work the jar, reciting the chant from step 10 three times.

13. When the jar is full, clean the money and spend it on a reward for your customers to thank them for loyalty.

Home and Family Jars

Jars are also useful in addressing matters of the home and family.

PROTECT THE PEACE IN THE FAMILY

The goal of this jar is to maintain peace in the home. This jar will not prevent fights, but it will help keep the atmosphere happy, healthy, and peaceful.

Don't worry if a full family photo is not available. Individual photos of each family member will work for this spell.

MATERIALS
- Family photo that includes everyone in the family
- Pen
- Small glass jar with a secure lid
- Dirt from your home
- 2 pieces of paper
- Pen
- 1 tablespoon dried chamomile (for peace)
- 1 tablespoon dried peppermint (for relaxation)
- 3 tablespoons dried rosemary (for family needs)

- 1 tablespoon dried lavender (for family love, peace)
- 1 tablespoon dried angelica root (for protection)

WORKING

1. On the back of the photo, write out the name and date of birth of everyone. As you write the information, focus on your love for the family and direct that energy into the photo. Place the photo in the jar facing up.

2. Cover the photo with the dirt from your home.

3. Use the pen and paper to write out a petition, following the directions from part 1. Fold the sheet of paper with the final petition in half toward you, then place it into the jar.

4. Add each of the herbs, and state why you are using them as you do:

   Chamomile for peace and hope.

   Peppermint for peace of mind.

   Rosemary for the home and family.

   Lavender for peace and calm emotions.

   Angelica root to protect the peace and love of this home.

5. Seal the lid, and shake the jar. As you shake the jar, chant:

   Peace within the family. Peace to live happily.

6. When you feel that the jar has been charged enough, place it on a shelf behind a family portrait. Work the jar twice a week to maintain

the peace. If a fight occurs, work the jar two to three times a day.

7. Dispose of the jar when you no longer feel the need for it.

EASE COMMUNICATION JAR SPELL

Use this jar spell when both parties want to try to communicate but are having difficulties getting their views across clearly.

MATERIALS
- Pen
- 2 pieces of paper
- Glass jar with a secure lid
- Lapis lazuli tumble (for communication)
- 1 tablespoon dried eyebright (to opens eyes)
- 1 tablespoon dried lavender flowers (for love, peace)
- Sodalite tumble (for communication)

WORKING
1. Using the pen and paper, write your petition, including the names of the individuals who are having a difficult time communicating, following the method detailed in part 1. Fold the perfected petition in half toward you and put it in the jar.

2. Add the lapis lazuli to the jar. State:

> *Lapis to open the way for communication today.*

3. Add the herbs, and state why you are using each of the herbs:

> *Eyebright to see the point coming from me.*
>
> *Lavender for tranquility to communicate freely.*

4. Place the sodalite tumble into the jar, stating:

> *Sodalite to make communication right.*

5. Seal and shake the jar. As you shake the jar, recite the following chant three to five times:

> *By your words and mine, the solution we shall find.*

6. Place the jar on a shelf that is hidden but easy to find and work with. Once a day, shake the jar and repeat the same chant from step 5 five to seven times. Work the jar daily until the misunderstanding or miscommunication is cleared. Once that happens, dispose of the petition and the herbs, and cleanse the crystals and jar.

PET'S WITCHES' JAR

Use this witches' jar to protect your pet. If you have more than one pet, include an image or personal effect for each pet.

MATERIALS
- Glass jar with a secure lid
- Personal effects from your pet such as shed fur, skin, feathers, or whiskers

- ¼ cup cat litter or salt (to absorb and neutralize attacks)
- Nail clippings, shed claws, or 5 pins or needles (to attack negativity)
- 3 to 5 mirror fragments (to reflect negativity back)

WORKING

1. Place the gathered materials from your pet in the jar. As you place the materials, state:

   This (personal effect) is (pet's name)
   and shall act as a decoy for (pet's name)
   against all magical attack.

2. Pour the cat litter or salt into the jar, stating:

   To absorb any and all negativity or magical
   attack sent their way.

3. Add the claws, nail clippings, or pins or needles, stating:

   To pin, tear, and attack all evil magic sent
   this way.

4. Place the mirror fragments in the jar, stating:

   To reflect and return the attack back.

5. Seal the jar tight. Shake the jar, stating:

   To protect (pet's name). No harm shall come
   their way. They are protected this day.

6. Bury or place this jar opposite of your witches' jar. When you move, or if a pet dies, safely break and dispose of the jar, and create a new one.

Baneful/Curse Jars

Remember to consider all of your actions before working any baneful magic. Only you can decide if the consequences of your actions are something you can live with.

CHAOS & CONFUSION JAR

The goal of this spell is to cause your target to have confusion and chaos in their life. This spell is best used when you feel someone's life is going too well despite all of the problems they stir up and cause others. The pain in the spell can be physical pain, or it can be an emotional pain.

MATERIALS
- Photo or drawing of your target
- Pen
- Glass jar with a secure lid
- 3 tablespoons poppy seeds (for chaos, confusion)
- 1 tablespoon dried stinging nettle (for baneful magic, reversal magic)
- 1 tablespoon whole black mustard seeds (for discord and strife)
- 1 tablespoon poke root (for chaos)
- 5 pins or needles (to symbolize causing pain, stabbing in the back, etc.)

WORKING
1. On the back of the photo or drawing, write down your target's name and any identifying information you can think of. Under the

information, write what they did to you and how you are connected. Fold the photo or drawing in half away from you and state:

> *Image of (target's name) you are (target's name).*
> *I grant you life to cause (target's name) strife.*

2. Put the image in the jar, then toss in the rest of the materials.

3. Seal the jar shut, and shake the jar vigorously, focusing all of your anger and frustrations toward your target into the jar. As you shake the jar, recite this statement:

> *Chaos and confusion come your way.*
> *The pain you caused me is returned to you*
> *times three. Trapped you will stay until*
> *you've changed your way. When your lesson*
> *is learned will your freedom be earned.*

4. Place the charged jar on your shelf. Work the jar twice daily until your target's lesson has been learned.

5. When your target has learned their lesson, dispose of the materials in a public trash can away from both your home and work and the target's home and work.

SOUR REVERSE JAR

Pickle juice and vinegar are used in spells to cause a target to have a bad day. By keeping your target in the vinegar or pickle juice, the energy of the liquid also causes other people to finally see what a sour person your target is.

MATERIALS

- Pickle jar or vinegar jar with some juice remaining and a secure lid
- Pen
- Paper
- 2 tablespoons galangal root (to return to sender)
- 2 tablespoons stinging nettle (for justice work)
- 3 mirror fragments (to reflect the work back at the sender)

WORKING

1. Using the pen and paper, write down some way to identify your target and what wrongs they have done. Tear up the paper.

2. Place the torn paper in the jar with the vinegar or pickle juice. Cover the paper with the herbs.

3. Add the mirror fragments.

4. Seal the jar, and work it two times daily until your target learns their lesson.

5. When your target has learned their lesson and justice is served, dispose of the jar outside your home.

BATHROOM JAR CURSE

This curse is used for someone you have a long-term grudge against. The goal is to cause everything possible to go wrong in your target's life. You will activate this spell every time the toilet flushes.

MATERIALS
- Glass jar with a secure lid
- Pen
- Paper
- Personal effect of your target or photo or drawing of them
- Your spit
- 3 tablespoons mustard seed (for discord, problems)
- 3 tablespoons asafoetida (to leave you alone)
- 5 drops lemon juice (to sour them)
- Toilet paper

WORKING
1. Using the pen and paper, write out your target's name and date of birth if you know it. Under their name, write the wrongs they did. Spit on the paper, then add it to the jar.

2. Throw in the herbs, and pour the lemon juice over the ingredients.

3. Tighten the jar's lid, and shake it vigorously. Focus your anger and frustrations into the jar with the intent to cause them harm.

4. The next time that you have to go to the bathroom to pee, bring the jar with you. After you are done peeing, unseal the jar, wipe yourself with toilet paper, and toss the used toilet paper into the jar.

5. Reseal the jar, and place it on top of the tank lid for the toilet. Every time the toilet is flushed, the jar is activated. When justice has been served, dump the contents of the jar into a public trash can away from home.

BOTTLE SPELLS

Bottles come in all sorts of shapes and sizes, which is why they are so adaptable for magical use. Craft stores even have bottles that are small enough to be worn as part of jewelry. Any type of bottle can be used in magical work—just be sure to cleanse the bottle before use.

There is often a question about using plastic bottles and if plastic inhibits the flow of magical energy. I have not found plastic materials to have any impact on magic. It is no different from any other materials. Using plastic containers helps keep them out of landfills.

Protection Bottle Spells

Protection magic is a common form of magical work. This magical protection can be used for both physical protection as well as spiritual protection.

SAFE TRAVELS BOTTLE

This bottle spell is done to protect people while they are traveling. As long as this bottle remains with the person traveling, they will have safe travels.

MATERIALS
- Pen
- 2 pieces of paper
- 8-ounce bottle with cap
- 1 tablespoon dried angelica root (for angelic protection)
- 1 tablespoon dragon's blood resin (for protection)
- 1 tablespoon dried nettle leaves (for protection and to send negativity to those who cause accidents)

WORKING
1. Using the pen and a piece of paper, draft your petition. Rewrite your petition on the second piece of paper. Insert the petition into the bottle.

2. Add the herbs to the bottle. As you place each herb into the bottle, you can either state the name of each herb and "for protection" or you can recite:

*By the powers of the plant's lore, while I
(or traveler's name) drive/s (or travel/s)
protection is in store.*

3. Seal the bottle with its cap and start to shake it.
   As you shake the bottle, recite the Prayer to Saint
   Christopher three to five times:

   *Grant me, O Lord, a steady hand and
   watchful eye.*

   That no one shall be hurt as I pass by.

   *You gave life, I pray no act of mine may
   take away or mar that gift of thine.*

   *Shelter those, dear Lord, who bear my
   company, from the evils of fire and all
   calamity.*

   *Teach me, to use my car for others need;
   Nor miss through love of undue speed*

   *The beauty of the world; that thus I may
   with joy and courtesy go on my way.*

   *St. Christopher, holy patron of travelers,
   protect me and lead me safely to my
   destiny.*[3]

4. When you feel that the bottle has been charged
   enough, place it somewhere in the vehicle used
   for traveling. Once a week, work the bottle and
   recite the Prayer to Saint Christopher.

---

3. Jesuit Resource, "Prayer to Saint Christopher."

5. Dispose of the bottle when you get a new vehicle. Create a new bottle for each new vehicle you have.

EVIL EYE PROTECTION

Young children can easily fall victim to the evil eye as they are pure and defenseless. This protection spell can be used for children of all ages.

MATERIALS
- Paper
- Pen
- Baby bottle, preferably blue, with a cap
- Personal effects of the child or image of them (to act as a decoy)
- 2 tablespoon dried angelica root (for protection against curses)
- 2 tablespoon dried anise seed (to ward against the evil eye)
- 4 small blue fluorite tumbles (for protective nature and to repel evil)
- 4 pieces of blue sea glass (to repel the evil eye)

WORKING
1. Use the pen to write the child's name and date of birth on the piece of paper. If the child is in foster care, write down the date the child came into the care. If the child was adopted, write down the date of the adoption. Under their name and the date, write out: "Protection against the evil eye."

2. Place the petition from step 1 and the personal effects into the bottle. As the personal effects are added, state:

> *You are the (personal effect) of (child's name).*
> *You are a decoy against the evil eye sent to*
> *(child's name).*

3. Add the remaining materials to the bottle.

4. Seal the bottle tight and shake it to mix the materials. As you shake the bottle, recite Psalm 140:1–13:

> *Deliver me, O Lord, from evil men;*
> *Preserve me from violent men,*
>
> *Who plan evil things in their hearts;*
> *They continually gather together for war.*
>
> *They sharpen their tongues like a serpent;*
> *The poison of asps is under their lips. Selah*
>
> *Keep me, O Lord, from the hands of the wicked;*
> *Preserve me from violent men, Who have*
> *purposed to make my steps stumble.*
>
> *The proud have hidden a snare for me,*
> *and cords; They have spread a net by*
> *the wayside; They have set traps for me.*
> *Selah*
>
> *I said to the Lord: "You are my God; Hear*
> *the voice of my supplications, O Lord.*
>
> *O God the Lord, the strength of my salvation,*
> *You have covered my head in the day of battle.*
>
> *Do not grant, O Lord, the desires of the*
> *wicked; Do not further his wicked*
> *scheme, Lest they be exalted. Selah*

> *As for the head of those who surround me,*
>   *Let the evil of their lips cover them;*

> *Let burning coals fall upon them;*
>   *Let them be cast into the fire, Into deep*
>   *pits, that they rise not up again.*

> *Let not a slanderer be established in the earth;*
>   *Let evil hunt the violent man to overthrow him.*

> *I know that the Lord will maintain*
>   *The cause of the afflicted, And justice for*
>   *the poor.*

> *Surely the righteous shall give thanks to*
>   *Your name; The upright shall dwell in*
>   *Your presence.*

5. When you have finished reciting the psalm, place the bottle in a bag that you or the child will carry at all times when out and about. Remake the bottle once a year as long as you fear the possibility of the evil eye. Using the same bottle each time will produce the best results.

PROTECT YOUR LOVED ONE FAR AWAY

This spell was written to protect one of my closest friends while they served in the military. I used a Coke bottle with their name on the wrapper, but any bottle will work. You can modify this spell to work with other prayers and spirits.

MATERIALS
- Photo or drawing of your loved one
- Pen

- Tape
- 16-ounce bottle with a cap
- Your breath
- 2 tablespoons dried angelica root (for protection)
- 1 cup salt (to absorb negativity and ill will)
- 5 snowflake obsidian tumbles (for protection)
- 5 pieces of devil's shoestring (to tangle and trap ill will, trip up evil)
- 1 packet of clear seed beads (to confuse any evil sent their way)
- 5 pins or needles (to attack and trap any evil and negativity)

WORKING

1. On the back of the photo, write your loved one's name and date of birth.

2. Tape the photo to the bottle, then breathe over the bottle and state:

   Bottle you shall work as a decoy for (loved one's name) against ill will near and far.

3. Add the remaining materials in any order. As you add each item, think about your loved one being protected.

4. Seal and shake the bottle. While shaking the bottle, recite the Prayer to Saint Michael the Archangel:

   St. Michael the Archangel, defend us in battle. Be our defense against the wicked-ness and snares of the Devil. May God rebuke him, we humbly pray, and do thou, O Prince of the heavenly hosts, by the

power of God, thrust into hell Satan, and
all the evil spirits, who prowl about the
world seeking the ruin of souls. Amen.[4]

5. Place the bottle somewhere safe where you can work it twice daily. Once a month, recharge the bottle by shaking it and reciting the prayer three times. Continue this process for as long as they need the extra protection.

PROTECT AGAINST ANGRY CUSTOMERS

Use this spell when you had an unsatisfactory experience with a customer or client and think they may blame you for their poor experience.

MATERIALS
- Pen
- Paper
- Red pin
- Small glass bottle with a cap
- 1 tablespoon stinging nettle (for protection)
- 1 tablespoon stop sign dirt (to stop actions)
- 1 tablespoon dirt from your business property

WORKING
1. Using the pen, write "Stop Angry Customer" on the paper.

---

4. St. Michael the Archangel Roman Catholic Church. "Prayer to St. Michael the Archangel."

2. Tear those words from the paper. Fold the piece with the words in half.

3. Stab the paper with the pin, stating:

   Your experience poor, speak of never more.

4. Put the paper and pin in the bottle.

5. Add the stinging nettle and dirt to the bottle.

6. Seal the bottle, and shake it. Recite the previous charm five times. If possible, bring the bottle to work and hide it someplace. Work the bottle two times daily for the next two weeks. After two weeks, dispose of the bottle.

Message in a Bottle Spells

A common item included in seaside tales is a message in a bottle. In magic, we can turn that image into power for our spells both symbolically and literally.

TOXIC TRAITS BE GONE BOTTLE

There are times when we engage in toxic behavior. Use this spell to remove the energetic hold these traits have on you so you can begin to heal and change.

MATERIALS
- Pen
- Paper
- Scissors

- Small glass bottle with a cap
- 2 tablespoons black pepper (for banishment, removal)
- 1 tablespoon shaved horseradish (for banishment, removal)
- 1 tablespoon hyssop (for cleansing, protection)
- 1 tablespoon lemon balm (for cleansing)
- 1 teaspoon valerian root (for banishing, protection, removal)
- Ocean tide turning from high to low or a river flowing away from you

WORKING

1. Use the pen to write a list of your toxic traits and behaviors on the paper, leaving space between each trait and behavior. Use the scissors to cut the paper into small slips with each trait or behavior on a slip.

2. Place each slip into the bottle, stating:

   Trait begone. It's time to move along.

3. Cover the slips of paper with the pepper and herbal materials. Add them in any order, stating what you want from each of them.

4. Seal the bottle and shake it seven times, reciting the same trait begone statement.

5. Place the bottle where it will be hidden and undisturbed. Work the bottle two to three times daily for a month.

6. At the end of the month, bring the bottle with you to either a river flowing away from you or an ocean turning from high to low tide. Throw the bottle into the water and watch it drift away from you. If the ocean or a river is not available, take the bottle away from home and destroy it.

DREAM SEA SPELL

This spell sends your dreams and goals out across the world to manifest.

MATERIALS
- Pen
- Paper
- Glass bottle with a cap
- 2 tablespoons dried catnip (for happiness, hopefulness, joy)
- 2 tablespoons dried marigold flowers (for happiness, healing, joy, protection, success)
- 2 tablespoons dried sunflower seeds and petals (for happiness, joy, success)
- Ocean tide turning from high to low or a river flowing away from you

WORKING
1. Use the pen to write down what all of your dreams and goals are on the paper. These can be personal, professional, and life goals. As you write each dream and goal, see yourself achieving that dream and realizing that goal. Direct the

images and emotions into the paper. Roll the paper up and place it in the bottle.

2. Add the remaining materials, focusing on your dreams being protected and becoming a reality. As you add each item, state:

To manifest dreams come true.

3. Seal the bottle. Shake it joyously, filling it with the joy and fulfillment you will have as you accomplish your dreams. As you shake the bottle, recite the following chant seven times:

Dreams come true bring joy and cheer too.

4. Place the bottle somewhere you will see it daily. Two to three times daily for the next month work the bottle, reciting the chant from step 3.

5. At the end of a month, bring the bottle with you to a river flowing toward your home or an ocean moving from low to high tide. Toss the bottle into the water. As the bottle drifts away know it will bring your dreams across the world. As the tides move the bottle, the bottle is activated. If neither source of water is available, keep the jar on a high shelf in your home and work it two to three times daily to bring the joy into your life.

Money & Luck Bottle Spells

These spells help address a few specific issues regarding money or luck.

FAST CASH MONEY BOTTLE

Use this bottle spell for when you need to have money quickly. This spell is for emergencies. Use alternative methods for long-term, secure income.

MATERIALS
- 9-ounce bottle with a cap
- 2 pieces of paper
- Pen
- Tape
- 5 small coins of assorted value
- 3 iron pyrite tumbles (for desire, money, success)
- 2 goldstone tumbles (for money)
- 2 tablespoons dried alfalfa (to attract money)
- 2 tablespoons dried cinquefoil (for fast cash)
- 3 magnets (for attraction)

WORKING
1. Use the pen to write "Fast Cash Bottle" on one piece of paper. Tape that piece of paper to the bottle with the words facing out. On the other slip of paper write "Attract Money Quickly." Under the words, write why you need the money. Fold the paper and place it in the bottle.

2. Add the coins to the bottle. As you add each one, state:

   To attract cash quickly.

3. Add the iron pyrite and goldstone. As you add each stone, state:

   For money and luck.

4. Add the dried alfalfa and cinquefoil to the bottle. As you add them, state:

   Money and cash to me flows quickly and fast.

5. Add the magnets. As you add each magnet, state:

   To attract to me cash quickly.

6. Seal the bottle and shake it. As you shake the bottle, recite the following chant five to seven times:

   Cash flow quickly for I need money.

7. Place the bottle on a shelf in your living room where it will be undisturbed and unseen. Each day in the morning, before starting your day, work the jar, reciting the chant three to five times. Before bed, work the bottle again, reciting the chant three to five times more.

8. Work the spell until your cash need has been met. Once it has, dispose of the contents outside of your home.

BOOST YOUR LUCK BOTTLE

Use this bottle to boost your luck. If you enter luck-based contests or gamble, working this bottle will increase your chances of winning.

MATERIALS
- Pen
- 3 pieces of paper
- Blue nail polish or blue permanent marker
- 9-ounce bottle with a cap
- 2 tablespoons dried basil (for luck)
- 1 cinnamon stick or 1 tablespoon cinnamon chips (for luck, prosperity)
- 1 tablespoon dried clover (for luck)
- 2 tablespoons dried pine needles (for luck, prosperity)
- Piece of iron pyrite (for luck)
- Magnet (for attraction)

WORKING
1. Use the pen to draft a petition and design a sigil on a piece of paper. Write out the final petition and sigil on the remaining two pieces of paper. Place them in the bottle. Draw the sigil on the bottle cap with the nail polish or permanent marker.

2. Add all of the herbs and state:

   Lucky me brings prosperity.

3. Add the iron pyrite and magnet to the bottle.

4. Seal the bottle, then shake the bottle and recite the following chant five to seven times:

Lucky me brings prosperity.

5. Place the bottle where you won't forget it. Before you enter a luck-based contest or spend some time gambling, work the container, reciting the same chant from step 2 and 4 three to five times. Recharge the bottle monthly as needed to keep your luck boosted. Dispose of the contents when you see fit.

ATTRACT LOYAL CUSTOMERS BOTTLE

Use this bottle to continue to increase your customer and client base which will improve sales.

MATERIALS
- Small bottle with a cap
- Pen
- 3 pieces of paper
- Tape
- Dirt from your business property
- 5 small magnets (for attraction)
- 5 tablespoons sugar, divided (for attraction)
- 2 tablespoons aloe vera juice (for prosperity, success)
- 1 tablespoon fresh or dried goldenrod flowers (for money)
- 1 teaspoon ground nutmeg (for luck, money, prosperity)

- 2 tablespoons fresh or dried marigold flowers (for luck, prosperity, success and to protect your money)

WORKING

1. Use the pen to draft a petition and sigil for an increased loyal customer base on a piece of paper. Copy the final petition and sigil onto the second piece of paper. Draw a clean copy of only the sigil on the third piece of paper. Tape the third paper to the bottle with the sigil facing out. Roll the second paper up and stick it in the bottle.

2. Add the dirt to the bottle, stating:

   Dirt from my business floor, attract customers to our door.

3. Place each magnet into the bottle. Between each magnet, add 1 tablespoon of sugar, stating:

   Sweetly attract customers who lovingly come back.

4. Add the remaining materials in any order, telling each item why it is used as it gets added.

5. Seal the bottle, and shake it enthusiastically. While shaking the bottle, recite this chant five to seven times:

   Every customer I see brings their friends to me.

6. Bring the bottle to your shop or office, and keep it hidden. Work the bottle two times daily, once at the start of the day and again at the end of the

day, repeating the chant from step 5 seven times.
Feed the bottle weekly. Recharge it monthly as
needed. Dispose of the bottle when you see fit.

Health and Healing Bottles

Healing magic is something I am passionate about, and it was
where I got my start in magical work. You can use these two
healing spells as supplements to normal medical treatments.

PROMOTE HEALTH
& WELLNESS BOTTLE

Use this bottle to promote health and wellness for
an individual. This spell works with a used pill,
supplement, or vitamin bottle. What matters is that
the bottle contained a pill of some sort. The small
quartz chips used in this spell can be found at most
craft stores.

MATERIALS
- Used pill, supplement, or vitamin bottle with a cap
- Small mixing bowl and spoon or mortar and pestle
- 2 tablespoons dried allheal (for healing)
- 2 tablespoons dried lavender (for healing)
- 2 tablespoons dried chamomile (for healing)
- 2 tablespoons dried marigold (for healing)
- Small jewelry-sized quartz chips (for power boost)

WORKING

1. Thoroughly wash and cleanse your bottle, removing the label completely.

2. Mix the herbs in the bowl or mortar. While mixing the herbs, visualize blue light coming from the herbs. As you mix, recite this chant three to five times:

   Health and wellness come to thee.
   Healing you so shall it be.

3. Pour the mixture into the bottle. Top the bottle off with the quartz chips.

4. Seal and shake the bottle, reciting the chant from step 2 three to five times.

5. Carry the bottle in your purse or bag daily, and work it as needed, reciting the chant three to five times. If you do not carry a purse or bag, place the bottle somewhere you will have it with you every day.

6. Recharge this bottle once a month as needed. When you no longer feel the need for this health boost, dispose of the materials appropriately. Recycle the bottle or set it aside to be washed and used in other spells.

PORTABLE HEALING CHARM

Everyone has something that they can use healing from, and the charm focuses on providing whatever healing energy is needed at the time.

MATERIALS

- Old supplement or over-the-counter medication bottle with a cap
- Pen
- 3 slips of paper
- Tape
- Blue nail polish or blue permanent marker
- 3 tablespoons dried allheal (for healing)
- 1 tablespoon dried angelica root (for health and to protect health)
- 1 tablespoon coriander seeds (for healing)
- 2 tablespoons ground ginseng or ginger (for healing)
- 2 tablespoons dried lavender (for healing)
- Small quartz tumble (for power boost)
- Small amethyst tumble (for healing)

WORKING

1. On one slip of paper, use the pen to draft a petition for a general healing boost. Use that petition to draft a sigil on the same piece of paper. On the second piece of paper write the final petition and sigil. Roll it up and slide it into the bottle. On the third piece of paper, write "Healing Boost." Draw your sigil under those words. Tape the third piece of paper to the bottle with the words and sigil facing out. Use the nail polish or permanent marker to draw your sigil on the bottle cap.

2. Add all of the remaining materials in any order. As you add each item, state why it has been chosen and what you want it to do. While you

add each item to the bottle, visualize a pale blue healing light filling the bottle. The light should grow brighter and more powerful with each item added.

3. Seal the bottle tightly. Shake the bottle with love and care, mixing the materials thoroughly. As you shake the bottle, recite the following chant seven to nine times:

> *Herbs of healing might, bless me with your healing light.*

4. Find a way to carry the bottle with you at all times, and work the bottle two to three times daily, reciting the same chant. Feed the bottle with healing oils and incense weekly. Recharge once a month as needed.

Spirit & Psychic Development

Spirit work and psychic development are common magical and spiritual practices. For effective spirit and psychic work, you must do the work yourself, but charms like this can be tools to help that practice.

MINIATURE ANCESTOR BOTTLE

This spell creates a small charm that you can wear, carrying the power and blessings of your ancestors with you wherever you want. You can find the recipe for ancestor incense in part 3.

MATERIALS

- Pen
- 3 tiny slips of paper
- Miniature jewelry bottle with a cap
- 1 pinch cemetery dirt from an ancestor's grave
- 1 pinch fresh or dried basil (for ancestor veneration)
- 1 pinch fresh or dried parsley (for ancestor veneration)
- 1 pinch fresh or dried patchouli leaves (for ancestor veneration, the dead)
- 1 pinch fresh or dried rosemary (to draws spirits and for family, love, protection)
- 1 pinch fresh or dried wormwood (for ancestor work, calling the spirits, love, protection, underworld work)
- 1 inch fine jewelry wire
- Necklace chain with a length that appeals to your style, taste, and way of life

WORKING

1. Use the pen to write, as small as you can, "Ancestors of Blood" on both sides of one slip of paper. On both sides of the second slip of paper write "Ancestors of the Heart." On the final slip of paper, write "Ancestors of the Spirit" on both sides.

2. Add the slips of paper to the bottle. Know that the ancestors of blood, heart, and spirit will be with you. Feel their love and protection surrounding you.

3. Add each of the herbs to the bottle, stating:

   For my ancestors.

4. Seal the bottle and shake it. As you shake the bottle, recite the following ancestor prayer three times:

   Ancestors of mine, protect me each day.
   Help me to find my way. From you may
   blessings of prosperity and strength stay.
   Blessed ancestors, I honor you this day.

5. Wrap the wire around the neck of the bottle and create a loop the bottle can hang from. Add the bottle to the necklace chain, and wear it proudly. Anytime you need to feel connection and protection from your ancestors, hold the bottle pendant.

6. Feed the bottle ancestor incense once a month by passing the necklace and pendant through the incense smoke five times while reciting the ancestor prayer. Recharge as needed during Samhain or other ancestor veneration rituals. When the pendant falls or breaks off, dispose of the pendant. Make a new one. The first one has finished working.

OPEN PSYCHIC EYE KEY BOTTLE

Use this bottle to awaken your psychic senses by holding it when doing divination or trance work. When you feel your senses are awakened and sufficiently developed, burn the herbs as incense and keep the key as a psychic charm.

MATERIALS

- Small bottle with a cap
- Skeleton key, which can be found at a hardware store, or a key without a lock (for unlocking senses)
- 1 to 2 feet of string
- 5 pieces of star anise seed (for psychic abilities)
- 2 tablespoons dried mugwort (for psychic gifts and to open psychic senses)
- 2 tablespoons dried marigold flowers (for psychic gifts and to open psychic senses)
- 2 tablespoons dried yarrow flowers (for psychic gifts and to open psychic senses)
- 5 small fluorite tumbles, preferably purple (for clarity of psychic senses)

WORKING

1. Set the bottle where you do most of your psychic development work. Sit down in front of the bottle and take a breath. Hold the key to your psychic eye (center of your forehead). State:

   Metal key, today open up the way.

2. Take the string and tie the key to the neck of the bottle so that the key is hanging inside the bottle along the neck.

3. Add the star anise seeds to the bottle. As you add them, state:

   To open psychic sight today, the seeds clear the way.

4. Add the remaining herbs in any order. As you add each herb, state:

   My psychic sight opens tonight.

5. Add the fluorite tumbles to the bottle. As you add each tumble, state:

   For clarity and insight of the senses that open tonight.

6. Seal the bottle. Hold the bottle to the center of your forehead and shake it well. As you shake the bottle, state the following chant five to seven times:

   Psychic abilities that are mine, awaken now it's time.

7. Place the bottle under your work area. Before you attempt to do any divination, meditation, or psychic work, hold the bottle to your third eye, and shake it three times. Then open the bottle and take out the key. Hold the key up to your third eye and state:

   Metal key today, open up the way.

8. Hold the key there for five breaths, then move the key from your third eye and hold it in one hand. Now begin doing your psychic development work.

9. When the work is done, retie the key to the bottle neck and place the bottle back under the table or workspace. Continue to work the bottle until you feel confident in your senses and abilities.

10. When you are confident in your abilities, empty the bottle. The herbs can now be burned as an incense during psychic work. Store the key with your divination tools. It is now able to open your psychic senses whenever you need it to.

SPIRIT CONNECTION BOTTLE

This bottle is to help you communicate and connect with your spirit guides. The more you work and attend to this bottle, the quicker your relationship with the spirits will develop.

MATERIALS
- Small bottle with a cap
- Celestite tumble (for spirit communication)
- 2 tablespoons dried angelica root (for connection to angels and spirits)
- 2 tablespoons frankincense resin (to act as a meditation tool, attract spirits)
- 2 tablespoons myrrh resin (to attract spirits)
- 2 tablespoons dried yarrow (for spirit communication)
- 4 small clear quartz tumbles (for aid and to boost power)

WORKING
1. Place the celestite in the bottle, stating:

> *For communication between my spirit guides and myself.*

2. Add the angelica root to the bottle. As you add it, state:

   For angelic aid in communication with my spirit guides.

3. Pour the frankincense and myrrh resins into the bottle, stating:

   Frankincense and myrrh to attract and honor my spirit guides.

4. Add the yarrow to the bottle. As you add it, state:

   For psychic and spirit communication.

5. Add the quartz crystals, stating:

   To boost the signal between my spirit guides and myself.

6. Hold the bottle to your third eye. As you hold the bottle to your psychic center, chant:

   To communicate freely between spirits and me; messages flow easily.

7. Focus on the sensations you get when you have contact with your spirit guides. Direct that energy and those sensations into the bottle. When the bottle starts to vibrate with spirit energy, place it on your altar, shrine, or workspace.

8. Next time you are trying to communicate with your spirit guides, hold the bottle in one hand as you communicate. Continue to use this bottle for as long as you feel the need for a boost. Once you no longer need it, empty the bottle, and burn the herbs as an incense offering to your guides. Charge or cleanse the crystals.

Curse and Hex Bottles

Bottles provide an interesting tool for baneful magic. You can destroy them, freeze them, and fill them with all sorts of nasty materials. Baneful magic with bottles can be done in a variety of ways, but before you cast these spells, you must check with your morals and ethics.

DROWN PROBLEMATIC INDIVIDUALS

This spell symbolically drowns those individuals who are causing you problems in your life. Vinegar is the best liquid for this, as it provides sour energy as well as being able to drown your petition.

MATERIALS
- Pen
- Paper
- 16-ounce bottle with a cap
- Your spit
- 3 pins (for pain)
- 1 tablespoon poppy seeds (for chaos, confusion)
- 1 teaspoon ground cayenne pepper (for fire energy, hexing, speed)
- 1 teaspoon dried nettle leaves (for hexing, justice and to return to sender)
- Approximately 2 cups vinegar (to act as a souring agent)

WORKING

1. Use the pen to write out how to identify your target on the paper. Under that information, list what wrongs they have done. Tear the paper, directing your anger and frustration into each tear. Spit on the torn paper and add it to the bottle.

2. Put the pins in the bottle, stating:

   For the pain you have caused.

3. Pour the herbs over the pins and paper.

4. Fill the bottle with vinegar. As you add the vinegar, state:

   I drown your name today. For your wrongs you must now pay.

5. Seal the bottle and shake it angrily. As you shake the bottle, recite this chant nine times:

   Chaos and confusion your way. For your wrongs you must pay.

6. Place the bottle in a dark corner of your house. Work the bottle twice daily, saying the chant from either step 4 or step 5 seven to nine times. Work the bottle until your target has learned their lesson. Dispose of the bottle when they have learned their lesson and repented for their actions.

FREEZE & SOUR

The goal of this bottle is to freeze your target, and it symbolically freezes them by freezing their name. You can add reflective materials to return their actions back to them.

MATERIALS
- Paper
- Pen
- 16-ounce bottle with a cap
- Water
- ½ cup lemon juice (for justice work, souring)
- ½ cup lime juice (for hexing, reversal, souring)
- ¼ cup apple cider vinegar (for souring)

WORKING
1. Use the pen to write your target's name and date of birth on the paper. If you do not know your target's name or date of birth, write some way to identify your target. Place the paper in the bottle.

2. Fill the bottle with water until half of the paper is covered.

3. Add enough of the remaining liquids to cover the paper.

4. Seal the bottle. Shake it to activate the souring component.

5. Place the bottle in a freezer. As long as the bottle remains there, your target will be frozen.

6. When you feel your target has learned their lesson and wish to release them from their freeze, take the bottle out of the freezer and let it thaw.

7. Flush the thawed liquid down the toilet. Take the bottle away from home and dispose of the remains.

Bottle Trees

The job of a bottle tree is to protect the home from evil by trapping the spirits within the bottles. Cobalt blue bottles are traditional for bottle trees, but any glass bottle can work.

APPALACHIAN BOTTLE TREES

Use this technique to protect your house from the evil eye and ill will sent your way. You only add to the tree when you feel that you are under attack.

MATERIALS
- 3 to 5 glass bottles, preferably blue or brown
- Dead tree, dead shrub, or collection of dead limbs
- Wire or string

WORKING
1. Once your bottles are cleaned and cleansed, take them out to the tree or shrub. Place the bottles on the branches. If the bottles do not stay secure, use the wire or string to secure them. Use the same process when working with dead limbs.

2. Once the bottles are secure, walk away. Listen for the sound of the bottles tinkling in the wind. That sound means you have caught evil sent your way.

3. Add a new bottle to the tree each day until the sensation that you are being attacked stops.

4. Once you no longer feel attacked, it is time to kill the spirits and dispose of the bottles. Cut and burn the branches and then safely smash and dispose of the bottles. Smashing the bottles kills the trapped spirits.

BALL SPELLS

Magical balls come in three forms: glass or plastic ornaments, dirt or clay balls, and jack balls. Each form of magic ball provides a unique twist on ball magic. One method is not better than the other. I will go over each method in detail, and I invite you to try each one and find the one that works best for you and your practice.

I'll begin with spells that use plastic or glass ornament balls, which are easily found. These balls are used to create unique ornaments that work powerful magic. Before I begin, there are several issues with this method that must be considered before working with these balls. First, the openings are fairly small, which limits the choice of fillings. (If you have trouble filling these balls, try using a funnel.) Second, these balls can become heavy. If they are too heavy, they won't hang as ornaments, and they will need another way to be displayed.

Another issue with this form of magical ball is the availability of materials. These glass or plastic balls are typically only available for a short period of the year around the December holiday season, although some big box craft stores stock them year-round. To ensure that you have these balls on hand, buy a large collection when they're available and store them for later use.

Traditional European Witches' Balls

Traditional European witches' balls attract and trap evil by using either reflective glass or clear plastic. Chords, twine, or tangled wire also work as a maze to trap and confuse spirits. The maze's confusion is compounded by the reflections. Finally, spirits also have to count every seed, bead, or salt grain put into the ball. Altogether, this creates a trap evil cannot readily escape. These traditional magical balls can be used as an alternative to witches' jars.

TRADITIONAL EUROPEAN WITCHES' BALL

This works as protection against baneful magic. The innocent ball traps evil and ill will, and the trapped spirits are forced to count the seed beads or salt within.

If you can't find jewelry wire, you can also use any thin wire, clear fishing line, or strong thread. It just needs to support the ball when hung.

MATERIALS
- 2 6-inch lengths of jewelry wire
- Clear glass or plastic ornament ball
- 1 small package of clear seed beads or 1 cup salt
- Hot glue gun and glue
- Silver or gold acrylic paint
- Paintbrush

WORKING
1. Twist and knot one length of wire. As you do so, make sure the length of wire is still small enough to fit inside the ball. Set it aside.

2. Pour roughly half of the glass beads or salt into the ball. Insert the knotted wire, then add the rest of the beads.

3. Use the hot glue gun and glue to secure the top of the ball to the opening. Set it aside and let it dry.

4. Once the glue has dried, use the paint and paint brush to add swirls or other attractive patterns to the ball. When you feel that the ball is decorated properly, set it aside and let the paint dry.

5. Once the paint has dried, use the remaining wire to create a hook to hang the ball from. Attach the hook to the ball and shake the ball gently to mix the materials inside.

6. Hang the ball in one of your front windows. Leave the ball there until you move to a new home. When you move, dispose of the old ball and create a new one.

American Folk Magic Witches' Balls

American folk magic practices have their own forms of witches' balls. Following are two types of these spells. The first is one commonly found along the coast of New England. These witches' balls are made from dark glass such as blue, green, or brown and crafted with lines that move like optical illusions. The second folk magic witches' ball is from southern Conjure. These balls use pins and needles to destroy the trapped evil.

New England Witches' Ball

This is a popular charm found along the New England coast. Hang this ball outside your home to protect against ill will, bad luck, and negativity.

MATERIALS
- Clear glass ball
- Light blue, light brown, or light green glass paint
- Dark blue, dark brown, or dark green glass paint
- Silver glass paint
- Paintbrush
- Small woven net to hang the ball from

WORKING

1. Use the paintbrush to cover the ball completely with a coat of paint. You can use either the light or dark color.

2. Once the first coat of paint is dried, take the second paint color and paint thin lines around the container that swirl from the bottom to the top.

3. Once the second coat of paint has dried, use the silver paint and brush to splatter dots all over the inside and outside of the ball. Set aside to dry.

4. Once the final coat of paint has dried, use the hot glue gun and glue to secure the top of the ball to the opening. Set it aside and let it dry.

5. Once the paint is dry, hang the ball in the woven net outside your home. As you hang the ball, state:

   Witches' ball trap today all that is unwanted sent my way.

6. Leave the ball hanging until you move to a new home. When you move to a new home, safely destroy the ball and create a new one for the new home.

SOUTHERN CONJURE WITCHES' BALL

This ball is a substitute for a witches' jar that protects your home against evil, ill will, and bad luck.

If you can't find jewelry wire, you can also use any thin wire, clear fishing line, or strong thread. It just needs to support the ball when hung. A clear glass ball is a perfectly fine substitution for a blue, brown, or green glass ball.

MATERIALS
- Blue, brown, or green glass ball
- Silver or gold acrylic paint
- Paintbrush
- 2 6-inch lengths of jewelry wire
- 1 package of clear seed beads or 1 cup salt
- 5 pins or needles
- Hot glue gun and glue

WORKING
1. Twist and knot one length of wire. As you do so, make sure the length of wire is still small enough to fit inside the ball. Set it aside.

2. On the outside of the ball, use the paintbrush and paint to add decorative lines.

3. Once the paint is dry, add the beads, knotted wire, and pins or needles to the ball.

4. Use the hot glue gun and glue to seal the ball.

5. Once the glue is dry, use the remaining wire to create a hook to hang the ball from. Give the ball a gentle shake to mix everything around.

6. Hang the ball in one of your front windows. Leave the ball in place until you move to a new home. When you move, dispose of the old ball and create a new one for the new home.

Modern Magical Ball Charms

Today you can find ball charms in occult shops for nearly any and all magical needs. Some people incorrectly label these charms as witches' balls when they are not. Even so, these are still powerful charms that can work effective magic.

ANCESTOR PROTECTION BALL

This ball brings the energy and protection of your ancestors into your home. This spell can be used even when ancestors are unknown; you can work with anyone who has passed that you consider an ancestor.

MATERIALS
- Ancestor incense (for an offering to your ancestors)
- Charcoal disc and censer/incense burner
- Matches or lighter
- Small glass ball
- 3 pinches cemetery dirt or 3 tablespoons dried finely ground patchouli leaves (for connection to the dead)
- 1 fresh or dried basil leaf (for ancestor veneration and spirits of the dead)
- ¼ cup salt (to repel unwanted spirits)
- 3 to 5 skull or plain white beads
- Hot glue gun and glue

WORKING

1. Use the matches or lighter to light the incense and place it in your burner of choice. As you light the incense, state:

   My ancestors, I welcome thee. This incense is an offering from me.

2. With the incense still burning, add the cemetery dirt or patchouli, basil, and salt to the ball.

3. Pass the ball through the incense smoke, filling the ball with ancestor energy.

4. Add the beads to the ball.

5. Use the hot glue gun and glue to seal the ball closed.

6. Gently shake the ball. While shaking the ball, hold on to an image of your ancestors protecting your home, creating a shield of some sort around it. As you shake and visualize, recite this chant three to five times:

   Ancestor power, protect me this hour.

7. Once again, pass the ball through the incense, reciting the following chant five to seven times:

   Ancestors, bless this ball. It is a home for you all.

8. Extinguish the incense. Place the ball somewhere in your home to do the work.

9. To connect to your ancestors using the ball, hold it in your hands and recite this prayer:

Ancestors of mine, protect me each day.
Help me to find my way. From you may
blessings of prosperity and strength stay.
Blessed ancestors, I honor you this day.

10. To feed, pass the ball through the ancestor
    incense while reciting the prayer from step 9.

PEACEFUL HOME BALL

This spell is based on a charm I created for my parents to bring peace and harmony into their home. You can use this ball to bring peace into your family home.

If you can't find jewelry wire, you can also use any thin wire, clear fishing line, or strong thread. It just needs to support the ball when hung.

MATERIALS
- Clear glass or plastic ornament ball
- 2 tablespoons dried lavender (for a peaceful home)
- ¼ cup dried rosemary (for peace in the home and to protect the home)
- 2 tablespoon dried rose petals (for love)
- 5 rose quartz chips (for family love)
- 5 clear quartz chips (to empower and enhance the materials within)
- Hot glue gun and glue
- 6 inches of jewelry wire

WORKING

1. Add the herbs and rose petals into the ball. As you add them, state:

   For a peaceful home and family harmony.

2. Add the rose quartz chips to the ball. State:

   For the love of family.

3. Add the quartz chips to the ball. As you add them, state:

   To power and enhance the materials within.

4. Use the hot glue gun and glue to seal the ball closed.

5. Once the glue is dry, use the wire to create a hook to hang the ball from and attach it.

6. Gently shake the ball to energize it. While shaking the ball, feel calming light energy fill the room. As you shake and visualize, recite the following chant three to five times:

   Light of peace shining bright, fill this home with your glorious light.

   Direct the energy into the ball, watching the light grow continuously until it fills the room. Once the light has filled the room, take your dominant hand and draw a peace sign or pentacle over the ball, sealing in the light.

7. Hang the ball in a window in your living room and let sunlight shine through it. As the sunlight hits the ball, the energy in the ball will be released into the room and throughout your home.

8. Once a day, take the ball down and shake it. As you shake the ball, recite the light of peace chant from step 6 three to five times. Continue to work the ball until the peace boost is no longer needed. When the ball is no longer needed, dispose of the contents.

BOOST HEALTH & WELLNESS HEALING BALL

This spell is to help boost health. Use this spell for when you or a loved one has been fighting off seasonal colds and generally haven't been feeling well. This spell draws out and removes the forces causing the sickness.

MATERIALS

- Clear glass or plastic ornament ball
- Personal effects such as hair, nails, and teeth (Photos and scraps of old clothes are good substitutes.)
- 1 cup honey (for attraction, health, wellness)
- 3 tablespoons black peppercorns (for protection from illness, removal of illnesses)
- 3 tablespoons ground cayenne pepper (for protection from illness, removal of illnesses)
- 5 drops eucalyptus oil (for protection from illness, removal of illnesses)
- ¼ cup dried lavender flowers (for general healing)
- Hot glue gun and glue
- 6 inches of jewelry wire

WORKING

1. Place the personal effects into the ball, stating:

   For the health of (person's name).

2. Pour the honey into the ball. As you pour it in, state:

   To draw illnesses into this ball today.

3. Add the black peppercorns, stating:

   To banish all illnesses that come our way, and to not allow illness to stay.

4. Sprinkle the cayenne pepper into the ball. As you sprinkle it in, state:

   With the power of cayenne pepper's heat, all illnesses sent will be beat.

5. Add the eucalyptus oil. As you let each drop fall, state:

   Eucalyptus oil, cleanse and clean, remove from us illnesses and the unseen.

6. Add the lavender flowers, stating:

   Lavender, heal today. With your help wellness shall stay.

7. Use the hot glue gun and glue to seal the ball.

8. Once the glue is dry, shake and flip the ball to charge the materials. As you shake the ball, visualize it filling up with a blue healing light, sending healing to your target. See the light growing from the ball and flowing from it to your target, enveloping them in the light. While holding the

visualization and shaking the ball, recite the following chant three to five times:

Health today, healing stay.

9. When you feel that the ball has been charged enough, use the wire to create a hook and hang the ball somewhere that you have access to regularly. First thing every morning and last thing every night, shake the ball and recite the chant from step 8 five times.

10. Work the ball daily for as long as you feel the need. When the illness has passed, take the ball apart. Dispose of the ball by tossing it into a trash can away from home.

OVERCOME OBSTACLES BALL

This spell works by symbolically opening doors and paths to help you reach your goals. This may mean that the spell works by going through the obstacles in your path, or it may work by finding another way to reach your goal, avoiding the obstacles altogether.

MATERIALS
- Clear glass or plastic ornament ball
- Paper
- Pen
- 3 tablespoons dried lemon balm (to open roads, cut and clear all blocks)
- 1 tablespoon dried basil (for block removal)
- 1 tablespoon dried dill (to bring in luck)

- 1 tablespoon dried woodruff (for overcoming adversaries and obstacles)
- Hot glue gun and glue
- 2 skeleton keys, which can be found at a hardware store, or keys without locks (to open locks in your way)
- 2 6-inch pieces of jewelry wire

WORKING

1. Use the pen to write "Blocks Busted" five times horizontally on the paper. Rotate the paper 90 degrees. Write "Roads Open" fives time across "Blocks Busted." Fold up the paper and place it in the ball.

2. Add the lemon balm to the ball, stating:

   Lemon balm, cut away all blocks in my way.

3. Add the basil to the ball. As you add it, state:

   Holy basil, on this day, remove all that stands in my way.

4. Add the dill to the ball. As you add it, state:

   I'm no longer stuck for dill brings me luck.

5. Sprinkle the woodruff into the ball, stating:

   To overcome obstacles and adversaries. For power and victory.

6. Use the hot glue gun and glue to seal the ball.

7. Once the glue is dry, wrap one of the wires around the neck of the ball and hang the keys from it. Use the other wire to create a hook to hang the ball from.

8. Gently shake the ball to energize the work.

9. Find a place in your home to hang the ball. Once a day, work the ball, reciting any mantras or chants you feel are appropriate. Continue to work the ball daily for as long as you feel the need. When the obstacles are gone, dispose of the ball.

Clay & Dirt Balls

Another form of a magical ball is made from clay, dirt, mud, and herbs that are mixed together and formed into a ball. Depending on the work, the balls are either left for a while and then destroyed or are destroyed immediately to release the magic.

PROSPERITY, LUCK & SUCCESS BALL

Once you have made this ball, you will sprinkle its remains around your home for prosperity and success.

MATERIALS
- Small mixing bowl and spoon
- 1 cup dirt from your home
- 1 cup cornstarch
- ½ cup flour
- 2 cups sugar (for attraction, luck, money, prosperity)
- 2 tablespoons ground cinnamon (for prosperity, success)
- 1 tablespoon ground ginger (for success)

- 1 tablespoon ground nutmeg (for luck, prosperity)
- Zest of 1 orange (for luck, money)
- ½ tablespoon ground dried pine needles (for fertility, financial security, money, prosperity, success)
- Water

WORKING

1. Use the spoon to mix all of the ingredients but the water in the bowl. As you mix the materials, see yourself having a successful and prosperous life with your financial needs met. Direct those images into the mixture while you stir. As you stir, recite the following chant five to seven times:

   Money and prosperity, come to me. I have financial security.

2. Gradually, add a small amount of water to the bowl. Mix the water thoroughly before adding another small amount. Continue to slowly add in water until the mixture becomes a dough.

3. Remove the dough from the bowl, and knead the dough three times while reciting the same chant from step 1. After the third time, begin to shape the dough into a ball. Continue to recite the chant while shaping the ball.

4. Once the ball has been shaped, set the ball aside to dry for 36 to 48 hours.

5. When the ball is dry, bring it outside and walk around the perimeter of your home. As you walk the perimeter, break the ball into small pieces,

reciting the same chant from steps 1 and 3. Continue this process until the ball is gone. Know that you just seeded prosperity around your home.

REMOVE NEGATIVITY BALL

This ball is used when a sudden sensation of negativity, stress, or anxiety overcomes you out of nowhere. The goal of this ball is to remove the negative energy and send it far away from you.

MATERIALS
- Small mixing bowl and spoon
- 1 cup cornstarch
- ½ cup salt
- 3 tablespoons dried sage leaves (for banishment, removal)
- 1 tablespoon powdered copal resin (for banishment, removal)
- 5 dried bay leaves, finely ground (for cleansing)
- 1 tablespoon ground galangal root (for reversal and to remove hexes and curses)
- Water

WORKING
1. Use the spoon to mix all of the materials in the bowl except for the water, reciting the following chant five to seven times:

    Herbs that cleanse and clean today, absorb and remove ill will sent my way.

2. Continue to recite the chant while slowly adding water to the mixture. Add water until the mixture reaches a doughlike consistency. Shape the dough into a ball.

3. Let the ball harden for 15 to 30 minutes. Once the ball hardens, begin to rub the ball over your body, starting at your crown and moving down to your feet, using downward motions. When you get to your shoulders, trace down one side, then move over and trace down the other side. Continue back down your center and hips.

4. Once you have traced over your whole body, take the ball outside and to a nearby crossroads. Destroy the ball at the crossroads, dispersing the negativity in all direction. Return home.

BULLY BE GONE BALL

Use this spell to overcome the feeling of powerlessness when dealing with bullies. This spell will help you regain control and stop their influence in your life.

MATERIALS
- Pen
- Paper
- Piece of dried masterwort root (for control, gaining power)
- Small mixing bowl and spoon
- 1 tablespoon ground cayenne pepper (for removal)

- 1 tablespoon woodruff (for overcoming adversaries)
- 3 pinches stop sign dirt (to stop behavior)
- crushed snail shell (to stop behavior)
- ¼ cup flour
- 1 tablespoon cornstarch
- Water

WORKING

1. Use the pen to write down the name of your bully on the paper. If their name is unknown, simply write "My Bully." Under their name, write "You have no power over me." Fold the paper over the master root.

2. Place all of the remaining materials except the water in the bowl, and use the spoon to mix well. As you stir the mixture, recite this chant three to five times:

    Bully be gone. I am strong. No more bully-ing me; from your power, I am free.

3. Add the water a little at a time. Stir and recite the above chant until the mixture is sticking together, forming a dough.

4. Once you feel the dough is malleable and sticking together, shape it into a ball around the petition and root. Do your best to get the entire root covered with the mixture. Recite the following chant two to three times, or until the root is completely covered:

    Bully be gone. I am strong. No more bully-ing me; from your power, I am free.

5. Set the ball aside to dry for 15 to 30 minutes.

6. Once the ball is dried, bring it to a stop sign where you can discreetly destroy the ball. As you smash the ball, state:

> *From your power, I am free. With harm to none so must it be.*

7. Return home feeling lighter and freer. Know you can now live without worrying about that bully.

HOT FOOT NEIGHBOR

This ball is used to cause a neighbor to move away suddenly. Use this when other methods of dealing with your neighbor have not worked. This works best when you and the target neighbor share a property border.

MATERIALS
- Pen
- Paper
- Scissors
- Mixing bowl and spoon
- 1 tablespoon dirt gathered from their side of your shared border
- 2 dried, crushed eggshells (to reverse ill will they have sent out back to them)
- 3 tablespoon ground cayenne pepper (to cause them to move quickly)
- 1 tablespoon cornstarch
- Water

WORKING

1. Use the pen to write the name and the address of your target on the paper. Under that information, write all the problems they have caused you and the neighborhood. Direct your anger and frustration into the paper.

2. Shred the paper with the scissors. Place the shreds in the bowl.

3. Add the dirt to the bowl. Use the spoon to mix the dirt and paper together.

4. Add the eggshells to the mixture, stating:

   To reverse back all that (target's name) has done, causing them to run.

5. Mix the bowl's ingredients well, adding in the cayenne pepper. As the powder is added, state:

   To cause (target's name) to move away hastily.

6. Add the cornstarch to the bowl and mix thoroughly.

7. Begin to slowly add water to the bowl until the mixture has a dough- or claylike feel. Form the dough into a ball. As you shape the ball, focus and direct all of your frustrations into it. While directing this energy, state:

   Move (target's name) away from here, never again to reappear.

8. Let the ball dry for 30 minutes. After 30 minutes, the ball is now ready to use.

9. The next time you go outside when your target isn't home, smash the ball on their side of the border. Rub the materials into the dirt so it looks like nothing happened and return home. Your target should move away within the month.

Jack Balls

Jack balls, another type of magical ball, come from Conjure. They are made out of petitions, curios, and yarn wrapped around the curios. You work jack balls by swinging them. To attract something, swing the ball toward you, bringing the energy toward you. When you want to remove something, swing the ball away from you, drawing that away from you. These balls are fed whiskey once a month, but any alcohol works. Incenses and oils are substitutes when alcohol is unavailable.

Traditionally, petitions and curios used in jack balls are soaked in urine. Urine works as a personal effect. Other personal effects, such as hair or clothes, can be used. After being soaked, the petitions and curios are wrapped with an appropriately colored yarn. By the time the process is complete, it should just look like a bundle of yarn with a tail of yarn sticking out.

The following spells are based on traditional works, but they have been modified to work without urine. The different roots and curios make each jack different. Experiment with these balls, or create your own.

CLEANSING JACK BALL

This is an effective work to remove energy from outside the home that you don't want inside. Use after work, errands, and outings.

MATERIALS
- Pen
- 2 pieces of paper
- 5 drops eucalyptus essential oil (for protection and removal from unwanted energy)
- Personal effects such as hair, nails, and teeth (Photos and scraps of old clothes are good substitutes.)
- 3 sprigs of fresh rosemary (for cleansing)
- 3 bundles of dried pine needles (for cleansing)
- 3 black peppercorns (for protection)
- 4 feet of white or silver yarn (for cleansing, purity)
- Shot of whiskey

WORKING
1. Use the pen to draft your petition on one piece of paper. Include specific trigger events that generate unwanted or negative energy. Write the final petition on the second piece of paper.

2. Anoint the petition with the eucalyptus essential oil. As you anoint the petition, state:

    Protection this day; that unwanted energy be sent away.

3. Place the personal effects on top of the petition. As you place the personal effects, state:

> *Items from me, draw to thee all my*
> *unwanted energy.*

4. Add the rosemary, pine needles, and peppercorns to the pile, stating:

> *Cleanse and clean, protecting from that*
> *which is unseen.*

5. Wrap the yarn around the pile, covering the bundle and leaving only a 6-inch tail. As you wrap the bundle, chant:

> *To protect from ill will and magic attack.*

6. Feed the jack the whiskey. As you feed the jack, state:

> *Jack ball, I feed you today to keep ill will*
> *and negativity away.*

7. Hang or place the ball behind or near your front door. Whenever you get home or feel unwanted energy clinging to you, work the ball. As you work the ball, feel that energy being sucked up and directed away from you. Once a month, feed your jack whiskey, stating:

> *Jack ball, I feed you today to keep ill will*
> *and negativity away.*

8. Every six to eight weeks, to cleanse or refresh the jack ball, soak the ball in a hot-water bath with a pinch of basil leaves, eucalyptus essential oil, and frankincense essential oil. Submerge the ball in the bath until soaked. Once soaked, take the ball out of the bath, and hang it where it belongs

to dry. Once the ball is dry, feed it and return to your daily life. When you no longer need the ball, unwind the yarn from around the materials and toss them in the trash.

LUCK GAIN BALL

Good luck and good fortune is one of the staple practices in magic. This jack ball attracts good luck to you and protects your good luck from souring into bad luck. *Work this jack weekly.*

MATERIALS
- Pen
- 2 pieces of paper
- Personal effects such as hair, nails, and teeth (Photos and scraps of old clothes are good substitutes.)
- Rabbit's foot (for luck)
- 5 pieces devil's shoestring (to trip up evil sent your way)
- 3 pieces whole allspice kernels (to attract good fortune and good luck)
- 5 feet of yellow, orange, or golden yarn (for luck, prosperity, success)
- Shot of whiskey

WORKING
1. With the pen, write out your desire to protect your family's good fortune and ensure future good luck on the piece of paper. If necessary,

write a clean version of the petition on the second piece of paper.

2. Place the personal effects onto the paper, and fold the paper over the personal effects, stating:

> *Personal effects of mine, protect my luck*
> *this time.*

3. Place the rabbit's foot on top of the personal effects and petition, stating:

> *Rabbit's foot for luck and speed, quickly*
> *brings the luck I need.*

4. Place the devil's shoestring across the rabbit's foot, stating:

> *Devil's shoestring, trip up and send away,*
> *that which tries to turn my luck on this day.*

5. Place the allspice on top of the devil's shoestring. As you place the kernels, state:

> *Allspice attracts fortunes and luck.*
> *With its power I am no longer stuck.*

6. Wrap the bundle with the yarn, leaving a 6-to-8-inch tail. While you are wrapping the yarn over the bundle, recite Psalm 1:1–6 five times, or until the bundle is covered with the tail:

> *Blessed is the man*
> > *Who walks not in the counsel of the ungodly,*
> > *Nor stands in the path of sinners,*
> > *Nor sits in the seat of the scornful;*
>
> *But his delight is in the law of the Lord,*
> > *And in His law he meditates day and night.*

He shall be like a tree
  Planted by the rivers of water,
  That brings forth its fruit in its season,
  Whose leaf also shall not wither;
  And whatever he does shall prosper.

The ungodly are not so,
  But are like the chaff which the wind
  drives away.

Therefore the ungodly shall not stand in
  the judgment,
  Nor sinners in the congregation of the
  righteous.

For the Lord knows the way of the righteous,
  But the way of the ungodly shall perish.

7. Feed the ball the whiskey, stating:

   I feed you today to bring good luck my way.

8. Work the ball at least once weekly by swinging the ball toward you while reciting this chant five to seven times:

   Good luck today. Good luck here to stay.

9. Feed the ball every four to six weeks with whiskey. When you feed the ball, state:

   Jack ball, I feed you today to bring good
   luck my way.

10. For as long as you work and feed your ball, you will have good luck. When you no longer feel the need for the extra luck, you may unravel the ball and place the items in the trash, releasing the spell.

Love Only Me

This ball is to be used when you want to take your relationship to the next level. The goal is to make your partner desire you and only you. Only use this spell after talking about the possibility of an exclusive relationship and with their consent. Doing this spell without consent is a work of control and domination.

Ideally the fresh rose petals used in this spell would be from a rose that your lover has given you.

MATERIALS
- Pen
- Paper
- Personal effects of your target or photo or drawing of them
- Personal effects such as hair, nails, and teeth (Photos and scraps of old clothes are good substitutes.)
- 5 cardamom seeds (for love, lust)
- 5 coriander seeds (for fidelity, love, lust)
- 1 tablespoon fresh or dried red rose petals (for love)
- 5 feet of red yarn
- Shot of whiskey

WORKING
1. Use the pen to write out your name and your target's name five times on the paper. Turn the paper 90 degrees, or sideways. Over the names, write "Love Only Me" five times. Rotate the paper another 90 degrees, and write another layer of "Love Only Me" five times.

2. Place your target's personal effects or photo on top of the petition. Place your personal effects on top of them. As you add your personal effects, state:

   Think only of me lovingly and lustfully.

3. Add the herbs in any order. Spread them evenly across the personal effects.

4. Wrap the yarn around the herbs, personal effects, and petition until there is only a 6-to-9-inch tail of yarn hanging from the ball. Begin to wrap the tail around the ball, reciting the following chant until the ball is completed:

   Love that's new, love that's true. Passion's fire alight, bring me love tonight.

5. Feed the ball, stating:

   Jack ball, I feed you today to bring love and lust my way.

6. Work the ball weekly by swinging the ball. As you swing the ball toward you, recite the same chant from step 4 five to seven times.

7. Hang the ball in your bedroom. Whenever you are going to meet with your target, carry the ball with you in a pouch or pocket.

8. Feed the ball every four to six weeks with whiskey. When you feed the ball whiskey, state:

   Jack ball, I feed you today to bring love and lust my way.

9. Work the ball until you have achieved your objective. Dismantle and dispose of the ball accordingly.

BOX, TIN &
CHEST SPELLS

Boxes are a large part of our lives. Everything seems to come in a box of some sort. As long as we have had shipping and trading, there have been boxes or chests of some form. They are practical ways to store and ship materials—and to use magic.

Boxes can be made with many different materials. Cardboard boxes are some of the most common in the world today, but wood, glass, ceramic, and metal boxes all exist as well. The type of box that you use for your magic largely depends on the materials you wish to place in the box and where you are going to keep the box.

Box Spells

Cardboard boxes can fall apart easily from use and simple wear and tear. The fact that these boxes are destroyed easily makes them particularly useful for works of removal, banishment, and destruction.

Some of the following spells involve using fire to destroy the box. For safety, perform all of these spells outside and be sure to have all the necessary safety equipment on hand.

BANISH FEARS & BAD HABITS

This spell is to help you deal with fears you want to face and habits you want to remove. This spell will help you overcome both your fears and bad habits.

MATERIALS
- Fire extinguisher or large container full of water
- Pen
- Paper
- Small cardboard box with lid
- 1 tablespoon ground cayenne pepper (for banishment)
- 1 tablespoon black pepper (for removal)
- 1 tablespoon powdered dragon's blood resin (for protection from your behaviors)
- Matches or lighter

WORKING

1. Prepare your outdoor workspace by setting the fire extinguisher or water nearby and clearing the area of any fire hazards.

2. Use the pen to write out your biggest fears and worst habits on the paper. Once they are all written, tear the paper into small pieces. Place those pieces in the box.

3. Sprinkle the two peppers over the paper. As you sprinkle, state:

   To banish away fears and bad habits today.

4. Add the dragon's blood resin, stating:

   To protect from their return, this herb I do burn.

5. Cover the box with its lid, angrily stating:

   Problems trapped within, this battle with you I win.

6. Situate the box in your outdoor workspace, and use the matches or lighter to set it on fire. As you watch the box burn, focus on your fears and bad habits never returning. Recite the following chant until the box is ash:

   Fire burns; never more do they return.

7. Once the fire has burned out and the ashes are cool, stomp down on the ashes. Then gather the ashes and toss them into the wind to disperse what's left into the universe.

ANCESTOR BOX

The goal of this box is to create a place where you have access to ancestor energy all the time. Any materials placed in this box will be charged with ancestor energy, and this box can add ancestor energy to any work you do.

MATERIALS
- Fire extinguisher or large container full of water
- Coffin-shaped box with lid (for ancestors and the dead)
- 1 to 2 teaspoons cemetery dirt from an ancestor's grave (for ancestors and the dead)
- Pen
- Paper
- Photo of ancestor, optional
- Scissors, optional
- Firesafe container
- Matches or lighter

WORKING
1. Prepare your outdoor workspace by setting the fire extinguisher or water nearby and clearing the area of any fire hazards.

2. Place the cemetery dirt in the coffin box. Hold your hand over the dirt, and say a prayer of thanks to your ancestors.

3. Use the pen to write a list of known ancestors on the paper. While writing the list, focus on memories with your beloved ancestors. Direct that

energy into the paper. If using photos, write your ancestors' names on the backs of the photos.

4. Tear the paper into small pieces and place them in the firesafe container. If using photos, cut them into small pieces with the scissors and place the pieces in the bowl.

5. In your prepared outdoor workspace, use the matches or lighter to light the paper and photos on fire. Let them burn completely.

6. When the ash from the burned paper and photos is cool, collect it and sprinkle it over the cemetery dirt. As you sprinkle the ash, recite this ancestor prayer:

> *Ancestors of mine protect me each day. Help me to find my way. From you may blessings flow my way. Blessed ancestors, in this dirt may your presence be felt. For this I pray.*

7. Once the ash has been added, place the lid on the box and hold your hands over it. Feel the power of your ancestors pulsating from the box. The box is now ready to be used as a conduit of ancestor energy.

8. To charge an item with ancestor energy, place the item into the box and cover it with the dirt and ash mixture. Work the box twice daily, reciting the ancestor prayer daily for a month at which point the item will be charged. For other spells, use the mixture the same way you would any other dirt.

When possible, add new cemetery dirt to the box to boost the ancestor energy. To recharge it, pass the box through the ancestor incense blend (see the resources section for the recipe) while reciting the ancestor prayer.

If you decide to dispose of the dirt, return the dirt to the cemetery where you got it. Thank the ancestors and cemetery spirits for the dirt and return home.

BIND A BULLY

This spell is for use when someone has been harassing or bullying you or your loved ones. Use this spell after trying to find other solutions. Before working the spell be sure that you have done nothing to them; if you have acted in a way to bring the bullying on yourself, the spell will backfire and cause you problems.

MATERIALS
- Pen
- Paper
- 1 foot of string (to bind your target)
- Small cardboard box with lid
- 5 pins (to symbolically pin your target down)
- 1 crushed crab shell (to back off your bully)
- 1 tablespoon dried woodruff (for overcoming adversaries)
- Scissors

WORKING

1. Use the pen to write down the name of the bully on the paper. If their name is unknown, write "My/(loved one's name's) Bully." Under those words, write down what type of bullying is happening.

2. Fold the paper in half. Tie the string around the paper and knot it. Wrap the paper with the string, reciting this chant until the paper is surrounded by string:

   String wound tight, bind this bully tonight.

   Secure the wrapped string with a knot, and place the paper in the box.

3. Place the needles on top of the petition, stating:

   For the pain you have sent this way, bound and pinned you will stay.

4. Sprinkle the crab shell and woodruff over the paper and pins, stating:

   Back off today, or for your behavior you shall pay.

5. Place the lid on the box and shake the box. Keep the box where it will be undisturbed. As long as the bullying continues, work the box twice a day.

6. When the harassment stops and they have learned their lesson, take the bound paper out of the box. Cut the bound paper, stating:

   From your binding you are free; now you must act hospitably.

7. Dispose of the remaining materials.

CURSE REVERSE BOX

Use this box when you know that you have been targeted by someone. This works best when you have an idea of who might have cursed you. The goal is for your target to be pinned in place, allowing them to face and receive that which they sent out.

When gathering the fire ants used in this spell, be sure to use gloves, only collecting ants that are already dead.

MATERIALS
- Small cardboard box with lid
- Aluminum foil (to reflect back what has been sent)
- Pen
- Paper
- 3 pins
- 3 tablespoons dried galangal root (for justice work and to return to sender)
- 1 crushed, dried crab shell (for reversal work)
- 5 crushed fire ants (for hex work)
- Clean, fresh egg (for curse removal and protection)

WORKING
1. Cover the inside of the box with the aluminum foil. Make sure all sides of the box are covered. When the foil covers the insides of the box, state:

   To reflect back a magical attack.

2. Use the pen to write "Curse Reverse" on the paper.

3. Pierce the paper with the first pin, stating:

   Who cursed me shall be pinned today.

4. Pierce the paper with the second pin, stating:

   For their actions they must pay.

5. Pierce the paper with the third pin, stating:

   Justice comes your way.

6. Place the pierced paper in the box, and add the galangal root, dried crab shell, and fire ants.

7. Place the box's lid and shake the box. As you shake the box, direct all the turmoil caused by the hex into it. Feel the effects of the hex being drawn from you into the box. While shaking the box, hold these sensations and recite the following chant three to five times:

   I return to you what was sent to me.
   From your ill will I am free.

8. Shake the box until you feel the flow of energy from you to the box slow. When the energy flow has ceased, place the box in a dark corner where it won't be disturbed. Work the box twice daily until your target has learned their lesson.

9. When your target has learned their lesson and the reversal work is no longer necessary, toss the box in a trash can away from your home or work. If your target is unknown, you may need to perform some form of divination to find out if they learned their lesson.

10. When you get home from disposing of the box, grab the fresh egg from your fridge. Take the egg and rub it over your body, starting at your crown

and moving down to your feet. Be sure to use only downward motions as you rub.

11. When your rubdown is complete, crack the egg into the toilet. Flush it down the toilet. As you flush it, state:

> *From this curse I am free. No more ill will stuck to me.*

Tin Spells

Small metal tins make wonderful storage containers for small, easy-to-lose items. Being small makes it easy to hide the containers, too, which makes them ideal for the workplace.

ATTRACT MONEY TIN

This spell is a general money attraction spell. As long as you carry and work the tin, you will attract money.

MATERIALS
- Small tin
- Gold or green paint and paintbrush or nail polish
- Slips of paper
- Small magnet (for attraction)
- Sugar (for attraction)
- Dimes or coins of equal value (for money)

WORKING
1. Paint the inside of the tin with dollar signs or other money symbols using the paint and paint brush or nail polish.

2. Use the pen to write "Attract Money" on each slip of paper and place the papers in the tin.

3. Add the remaining materials to the tin. Then close the tin, and shake it enthusiastically. As you shake the tin, chant:

> *Money comes my way.*
> *Prosperous blessings stay.*

4. Carry the tin with you everywhere, and work the tin two to three times daily for as long as you need to attract money. When you no longer need to attract money, dispose of the contents as you see fit.

CALMING FORCE TIN

The goal of this spell is to create an object that emits a soothing energy, allowing people to slow down at work and reassess what's going on.

MATERIALS
- Small tin
- Blue paint
- Paintbrush
- Paper
- Pen
- 2 tablespoons dried marigold (for hope)
- 2 tablespoons dried lavender (for peace)
- 2 tablespoons dried catnip (for happiness)
- 2 tablespoons dried spearmint or peppermint (for relaxation)

- 5 drops chamomile essential oil (for peace, relaxation)
- 1 pinch of stop sign dirt

WORKING

1. Use the paint and paintbrush to paint a peace sign on the outside of the lid and bottom of the tin.

2. With the pen, write "Peace, Calm & Serenity" on the paper. Fold the paper until it fits in the tin. As you fold the paper, chant the words you wrote three to five times.

3. Add the herbs to the tin one at a time. As you add the herbs, state why each herb is being added to the tin:

   Marigold for hope.

   Lavender for peace.

   Catnip for happiness.

   Mint for peace and calm.

4. Close the tin and shake it, mixing the herbs. While you shake the tin, recite this chant five times:

   Peace and serenity you bring to me.

5. After the fifth chant, open the tin. Add the stop sign dirt, stating:

   A pause this day, lets peacefulness stay.

6. Close the tin. Shake the tin, reciting the following chant five to seven times:

   Serenity today. Peace and tranquility stay.

7. While shaking the tin, feel yourself being at peace.

8. When you feel that the tin has been charged completely, anoint the lid with 5 drops of chamomile essential oil. Use your fingers to rub the essential oil over the tin, covering the tin with its power. As you rub, recite the following chant two to three times:

   I seal in peace, serenity, and tranquility.

9. Shake the tin again. As you shake the tin, repeat the following words seven times:

   Serenity today.

10. Place the container where you feel it will do the most good. Leave the container undisturbed until you need that boost of peaceful energy. Feed the container once weekly with 3 fresh drops of chamomile essential oil, rubbing the oil around and repeating the following words five to seven times:

    Serenity today.

11. When you need that boost of peaceful energy, work the tin. As you work the tin, feel the peaceful energy you stored within entering your body. Recite the same charm from step 8 and step 9 five to seven times, or until you're at peace. Dispose of the contents when you no longer need the boost.

COOL YOUR JETS TIN

This magical tin is to be used when you feel that someone is moving too fast and missing details. This spell will get them to stop and reassess before going forward, allowing them to fix mistakes and address problems.

MATERIALS
- Pen
- Paper
- Small metal tin
- 3 pinches stop sign dirt (to stop actions)
- 5 drops peppermint essential oil (for cooling off)
- 1 tablespoon crushed snail shells (to move slower, pause)
- 1 tablespoon fresh or dried lavender flowers (for calm, peace)
- Sprig of fresh rosemary (to open their mind)
- Mirror fragment (for reflection)
- Water
- A freezer

WORKING
1. With the pen, write out the name of your target on the paper. Under their name, write out what they are moving too fast on and why you feel they are moving too fast. Place the paper in the tin.

2. Sprinkle the stop sign dirt over the paper. As you sprinkle the dirt, state:

   To cause (target's name) to stop and pause.

3. Add the drops of oil across the materials, stating:

   To cool (target's name) jets.

4. Sprinkle the snail shells into the tin and state:

   *To stall (target's name) and prevent
   (target's goal) from into failure fall.*

5. Add the lavender, stating:

   *For peace of mind, so that their answers
   they may find.*

6. Place the sprig of rosemary over the herbs and
   shells. State:

   *To open (target's name) to see all the issues
   that there would be.*

7. Place the mirror fragment in the tin and state:

   *So (target's name) can see the problems
   ahead of thee.*

8. Add just enough water to cover the materials.
   Close the tin and shake it hard. As you shake the
   tin, state:

   *Cool down, (target's name), and you will see
   the problems and solutions in front of thee.*

9. Place the tin in the back of the freezer. Add a
   splash of water to the tin daily and work the tin.
   Continue the work until your target has learned
   what needs to be addressed and how to address
   it. When the problems have been addressed,
   remove the tin from the freezer, let it thaw, and
   dispose of the contents.

STOP GOSSIP TIN

This spell is used to stop people from spreading gossip. You can use it to stop people from spreading news about you or your life without your permission or knowledge.

MATERIALS
- Black pen
- Paper
- Red pen
- 5 pins
- Small metal tin
- 1 crushed crab shell (to reverse the gossip to them)
- 5 crushed snail shells (to stop them in their tracks)

WORKING

1. Use the black pen to write down the name of the person spreading gossip on the paper. If their name is unknown, write "Gossip Spreader." Under the name or title, draw a large "U" to represent a smiling open mouth.

2. Use the red pen to draw an "X" three times across the "U." As you draw each one, state:

   The gossip you spread is now being put to bed.

3. Stab each "X" with the pins followed by the two top points of the "U." As you stab the paper state:

   Your mouth is pinned tight until you set the gossip right.

4. Add the paper to the tin. Over the paper, sprinkle the crab shell, stating:

> *To reverse to you the pain your gossip does spew.*

5. Add the snail shells. As you add them, state:

> *To stop your ill words from being heard.*

6. Close the tin and shake it with all your anger and frustration directed into the action. While you shake the tin, recite the following chant five to seven times:

> *Your mouth is shut tight until the gossip is set right.*

7. Place the tin where it's hidden and you can work as needed. Anytime you hear of gossip from your target, work the tin, reciting the same chant from step 6 five to seven times. Work this tin daily until you notice the gossip stops and feel they have learned their lesson.

Chests

Chests are often associated with traveling or moving. There is also the common image of treasure chests containing precious jewelry or gold. One thing that most chests have in common is that they are made from strong and durable materials. This strength makes them ideal for semipermanent spells.

Another use of chests is to create a magical and ritual space. This space exists within, on top of, and under the chest. Inside the chest any materials relating to your personal practice could be stored. When the chest is opened, the sacred space is activated, and the work can begin.

PROTECT FINANCES & LUCK CHEST

The following spell uses the imagery of a pirate chest filled with jewelry and gold. Use this spell to protect your finances from theft and to increase your wealth through luck and new opportunities.

MATERIALS

- Small wooden or metal chest with lock (to secure your finances and luck)
- Green or gold paint
- Paintbrush
- 3 pieces iron pyrite (to bring in fortune and luck)
- 5 pieces devil's shoestring (to trip up any evil or ill will sent your way)
- 3 pieces whole allspice kernels (to attract good fortune and luck)
- 2 aventurine tumbles (for good fortune and success)
- ¼ cup dried marigold flowers (to protect money)
- 5 silver dollars or coins of equal value (to represent your wealth)

WORKING

1. On the outside of the chest, use the paint and paintbrush to paint symbols you associate with money and wealth. See yourself living a comfortable life. Direct that mental and emotional energy into the painting.

2. Once the paint is dry, place the iron pyrite in the chest. As you place it, state:

   Fool's gold you may be; prosperity and luck you bring to me.

3. Place the pieces of devil's shoestring across the iron pyrite. As you place the pieces, state:

   Tangle, trip, and send away that which tries to remove prosperity this day.

4. Place the allspice kernels next to the iron pyrite. As you place the allspice, state:

   Allspice attracts fortunes and luck. With its power, I am no longer stuck.

5. Add the aventurine tumbles. As you place them, state:

   Crystals of green light, protect my fortune with your might.

6. Sprinkle the marigold over the chest's contents, stating:

   Flowers of marigold, protect my finances new and old.

7. Place the coins in the chest. As you place each coin, state:

   Coins bring to me money that flows abundantly.

8. Close and lock the chest. Shake the chest, reciting Psalm 1:1–3:

   Blessed is the man
   Who walks not in the counsel of the ungodly,

Nor stands in the path of sinners,
Nor sits in the seat of the scornful;

But his delight is in the law of the Lord,
And in His law he meditates day and night.

He shall be like a tree
Planted by the rivers of water,
That brings forth its fruit in its season,
Whose leaf also shall not wither;
And whatever he does shall prosper.

9. Place the chest somewhere that won't be disturbed. Work the chest daily to protect your fortune.

HOPE CHEST

This is a variation on a hope chest. This chest works as a reminder of your accomplishments, goals, and the everyday things that give you enjoyment. It is a simple yet powerful tool for manifestation.

MATERIALS
- Small jewelry chest
- Paint
- Paintbrush
- Materials to decorate the outside of the box, such as additional paint, glitter, feathers, and stickers
- Scissors
- Magazines

WORKING

1. On top of the jewelry chest, use the paint and paintbrush to write "Hope Chest." As you paint those words, think about your dreams, goals, and hopes. Direct your hopeful energy into your painting.

2. Decorate the rest of the chest with the remaining materials. When the box has been decorated to your liking, set it aside.

3. Go through the magazines and use the scissors to cut out three to five images that represent your goals. Place all the images in a small pile. Focus on the joy these dreams have for you.

4. Place the clipped images in the bottom of the chest. Close the lid, and shake the chest gently. While you shake the chest, chant:

   Hope box of mine, protect these dreams divine. In time they all shall be mine.

5. Place the chest where you will see and work it daily. As you work the chest, recite this chant three to five times:

   To give my dreams power, I charge them this hour.

6. Whenever you feel depressed, look through the chest and remember the joy it has for you. Then place the lid on the box and shake it three to five times before placing it back in its spot. When you accomplish a dream or goal, remove the image related to the dream or goal, and know you can make them all reality.

PROTECT HOME & FAMILY
WHILE AWAY FROM HOME

This spell is for when you will be away from home for two or more months. For this spell to be the most effective, you want a small chest, such as a jewelry box, that can easily be protected and padded by your clothes as you travel.

MATERIALS
- Small jewelry chest
- 1 tablespoon dried angelica root (for protection)
- Photograph or drawing of your home (to act as a personal effect, represent the spirit of your home)
- Pen
- Small amount of dirt from your home (for physical connection to the home and to represent spirit of the home)
- Group or individual photos of your family members, including pets (to act as personal effects)
- 1 lilac branch cut into four pieces small enough to fit in your chest (for protection)
- 3 acorns (for strength)

WORKING
1. On the bottom of the chest, spread out the angelica root. Know this root will protect your home.

2. On the back of the photo or drawing of your home, use the pen to write "Protect My Home." Place the photo or drawing on the angelica root with the image facing up.

3. Sprinkle the dirt from your home over the image or images. As you sprinkle the dirt, see your home full of love and being protected. Direct that energy into the dirt.

4. On the back of the photo or photos, use the pen to write out the name and date of birth of everyone pictured. Under that information, write "Protect My Loved Ones." Place the photo or photos in the chest, facing up.

5. Place the lilac branches over the photo or photos in the shape of a cross. As you lay the branches, state:

   A shield to protect my home.

6. Place the acorns on top of and across the lilac branches. As you place the acorns, state:

   Oak strong and true, protect my home, I ask of you.

7. Close the chest and hold it tight. Feel your physical strength rising in your body as you hold it. When you can no longer hold this sensation, direct it all into the chest.

8. See a force field now surrounding the chest. Know that the force field around the chest is also around your home.

9. Once a week while you are away, repeat steps 7 and 8. When you finally return home, remove the acorns from the chest, place them somewhere on your property, and thank them for their protection. Dispose of the lilac branches and the angelica root. Use any individual photos in personal protection works.

NIGHTMARE CHEST

The goal of this spell is to turn the anger and frustration you have for your target into nightmares.

MATERIALS

- Small chest with lock
- Pen
- Paper
- 1 mandrake root (for nightmares)
- 5 pins (to pierce their protections)
- 1 tablespoon dried galangal root (for cursing, justice work)
- Zest of 1 lemon (to keep awake, sour dreams)

WORKING

1. Use the pen to write your target's name on the paper. Then wrap the paper around the mandrake root. As you wrap the paper around the root, state:

   Root of mandrake, with your screams, to (target's name) send nightmares for dreams.

2. Use the pins to secure the paper to the root. With each pin, state:

   To pierce (target's name) shields.

3. Place the pinned mandrake root in the chest. Sprinkle the galangal root and lemon zest over the mandrake root. While adding these two herbs, state:

   By these herbs' power, I send (target's name) dreams that are sour.

4. Close the chest and lock it. Shake the chest to activate the curse. Work the chest nightly before bed, visualizing your target having terrible nightmares.

5. When you feel your target has learned their lesson, dispose of the materials away from both your home and theirs.

Chests as Magical Areas

Chests can work as a shrine and focal point for communication with spirits or deities. These chests should be able to hold all of the tools you need to communicate and work with a spirit. Depending on your chest's size, you may need to find some substitutions. Unless you are actively doing work, the chest will appear as just a chest to everyone, and many people who live on the road use their chest as a portable altar or workspace.

CHEST SHRINE RITUAL

Use this ritual to create a portable altar or magical work area. Make sure the chest will fit comfortably in your storage space without problems.

You can alter this ritual to create a magical workspace for yourself, rather than a shrine or altar for a spirit. Instead of focusing on a deity or spirit, you can focus on your magical work. When working this altered ritual, use any incense or oil and objects that you feel a strong, powerful connection to or that helps focus your magic. All of your magical tools are then charged within the chest.

MATERIALS

- Heat resistant multicompartment storage chest, such as a tool chest or tackle box
- Charcoal disc and censer/incense burner
- Matches or lighter
- Incense sacred to the spirit (for a spirit offering)
- Anointing oil (to bless and consecrate the chest)
- White taper candle
- Candle holder
- Images that connect you to the spirit
- Statues or trinkets that represent the spirit
- Herbs, crystals, or other objects sacred to the spirit (for offerings, spirit communication)
- Small bowl
- Small cup
- Water

WORKING

1. Set the cleansed chest, incense and incense burner or censer, and candle and candle holder in your workspace.

2. Use the matches or lighter to light the incense, stating:

   I give this incense to you, (spirit's name), as an offering.

3. Anoint the candle with the oil, and light the candle. As you light the candle, state:

*By the sacred candlelight, a shrine for
(spirit's name) is being built tonight.*

4. Anoint the chest with the same oil you anointed
   the candle with. As you anoint the chest, state:

   *I consecrate this chest that it be a shrine
   (or altar) for you. May this chest become a
   symbol of our partnership and a place we
   can work together.*

5. Waft the incense smoke over the chest. As the
   smoke fills and surrounds the chest, state:

   *By incense smoke, this chest is blessed in
   your name.*

6. Using the candle holder, pass the candle over the
   chest, stating:

   *Candlelight, shining bright, turn this chest
   into an altar this night.*

7. Set the candle down. In one compartment, place
   the images and statues of the deity or spirit. Fill
   the remaining compartments with any tools or
   items you use in your work with this spirit. Make
   sure one compartment can hold the incense
   burner or censer, bowl, cup, and candle holder.

8. When everything except the incense burner or
   censer, candle holder, and cup is placed in the
   chest, close the chest. (If you have an offering,
   keep the bowl out, and place the offering inside
   of it.) Set the incense burner or censer, candle
   holder, and cup on the top of the chest. Pour
   some water into the cup and state:

> *I give this offering to you, that you know*
> *my intentions are true.*

9. When the incense and candle stop burning, store the remaining tools in the chest until you work with the spirit again.

SACHET & CHARM
BAG SPELLS

Sachets are known by many names. Some people call them charm bags, medicine bags, or mojo bags. Most sachets are small and easily carried. The ability for these charms to be discreet is one of the main reasons why they are so popular. There are sachet charms for almost everything.

Something that prevents people from experimenting with sachets is not knowing how to sew. You don't need to have any sewing experience to make one. It's actually quite easy.

Sewing a Basic Sachet

To sew a sachet, you need a piece of fabric; I recommend a piece that's 4 inches by 6 inches. Choose a color and material that align with your intent. You will also need a sewing needle and two sturdy strands of thread. Begin by threading the needle with one of the strands, tying a knot at the end of it. Then fold the fabric in half. Either direction will work, but I often recommend folding the fabric toward yourself if the spell is to attract something and away from yourself if you are going to remove something. The folding is part of the magical process.

When you fold the fabric, you can choose to fold it with the good side in, stitch it up, and then turn it right side out. This will create a more finished and professional looking sachet with the stitching hidden. Or you can simply fold the fabric with the good side facing out and stitch it up. When I first started to sew, I chose the latter. Remember, sachets don't need to be pretty. They just need to hold your materials.

Once you've folded your fabric, stitch up the two sides as best you can, leaving the top open. The second thread will be used to tie, not stitch, the sachet closed. Sachets are never stitched shut; stitching them shut changes them from sachets to packets.

Sewing sachets as a part of the spell adds a lot of power through your focused intent. You should try to sew your own sachet whenever possible.

If you are unable to sew or choose not to, you can also use a store-bought pouch. Many metaphysical stores sell sachets in a variety of sizes, colors, and materials. These sachets are well made and ready to use. There are several things to consider when choosing the right sachet for your work. When deciding on color, size, and materials, consider these questions: What is the goal and intent behind the sachet? How do you plan on carrying and working the sachet? What materials do you plan on putting in your sachet? Once you have taken these questions into consideration, you can choose the right bag for your spell.

Store-bought sachets can be charged without being sewn. To charge a sachet, anoint the sachet with incense smoke and oil. As you anoint the sachet, hold it tight and focus on the magical work you are about to do. Direct that mental energy into the sachet to charge it for the work ahead.

Love & Lust Spells

The next selection of spells is based on love and lust work. Do not target specific individuals with these spells. Targeting specific individuals changes the work from love work to domination work.

Eyes on Me Sachet

This charm is used to attract sexual attention when you are out and about.

MATERIALS
- Pen
- 2 pieces of paper
- 4-by-6-inch piece of fabric, preferably red

- 2 2-foot pieces of dark red thread
- Sewing needle
- ¼ cup eyebright (to open the eyes)
- Lock of your hair (to direct attention to you)
- 2 tablespoons dried damiana (for passion, sexuality)
- 2 tablespoons ground cayenne pepper (for passion, sexuality)
- 1 tablespoon dried rose petals (for attraction, love)
- 1 tablespoon dried mace (for attraction, sexuality)
- Carnelian tumble (sexuality)
- 1 tablespoon sugar (for attraction)

WORKING

1. With the pen, write out your desire for the sexual attention you are looking for on the piece of paper. Make sure you include your sexual preferences; otherwise, you might attract unwanted attention. If necessary, write a clean version of the petition on the second piece of paper.

2. Fold the fabric in half, and thread the needle with one piece of thread. Then stitch up the sides of the fabric, as explained in the basic instructions. While stitching, repeat this chant until both sides are stitched closed:

   All eyes on me. Set my desires free.

3. Hold the bag to your heart to fill the sachet with love. Then add your petition to the bag.

4. Add each of the other materials. As you add each ingredient, state why you are using that item.

5. Use the remaining piece of dark red string to tie the sachet securely closed.

6. Take the sachet in both hands and begin to play with it. As you play with the sachet, recite the following chant three to five times:

> *All eyes on mine. Dates and sex are easy to find.*

7. Carry the bag with you whenever you go out. Before you go out, recite the chant from step 6 three to five times while playing with the bag to activate the energy. When you find someone you are attracted to, play with the bag and silently repeat the chant three to five times. When you are ready to settle into a long-term or stable relationship, dispose of the materials within the charm bag. There are other charms for long-term relationships.

DOMINATE LUST SACHET

Use this spell when the desire between you and your partner has faded. It will reawaken desire. Remember, always get your partner's consent to work the spell first. It is a spell to be done only between partners, and it must be done with their participation or—at the very least—their awareness.

MATERIALS
- Small bowl
- 1 cup apple cider vinegar (for lust)

- 1 tablespoon crushed dried mace (for domination, lust)
- 3-by-3-inch piece of your partner's old clothing or red fabric
- 2 2-foot pieces of dark red thread
- Sewing needle
- 1 tablespoon ground cayenne pepper (to spice up desires)
- 1 tablespoon dried rose petals (for relationship, romance)
- 1 tablespoon dried lemongrass (for desire, passion, sex)
- Lock of your hair (to direct attention to you)

WORKING

1. Pour the apple cider vinegar and mace into the bowl. Soak the fabric in the vinegar and mace mixture.

2. Once the fabric is thoroughly soaked, bring it to your workspace and fold it in half toward you. Thread the needle with one piece of thread and stitch up the sides, as described in the basic sachet instructions. Do not wait for the material to dry first. Stitch the material when wet. Yes, this is messy, but spells and magic in Conjure are often messy.

3. As you sew the fabric, begin reciting the Song of Solomon chapter 7:6–12:

   How fair and how pleasant you are, O love, with your delights!

This stature of yours is like a palm tree,
And your breasts like its clusters.

I said, "I will go up to the palm tree, I will take
hold of its branches."
Let now your breasts be like clusters of the vine,
The fragrance of your breath like apples,

And the roof of your mouth like the best
wine. The Shulamite
The wine goes down smoothly for my beloved,
Moving gently the lips of sleepers.

I am my beloved's, And his desire is toward me.

Come, my beloved, Let us go forth to the field;
Let us lodge in the villages.

Let us get up early to the vineyards;
Let us see if the vine has budded,
Whether the grape blossoms are open,
And the pomegranates are in bloom.
There I will give you my love.

4. Once you've finished sewing, add the remaining materials. As you add each of them to the sachet, remind them that they are for enhancing the lust between you and your partner. When you place each material into the bag, feel the lust growing stronger and wilder.

5. When the sachet is full, take the remaining dark red thread and tie it shut. Let it dry, then carry it in your bra or front shirt pocket.

6. Once a week, feed the sachet by soaking or dipping it in a fresh vinegar and mace wash. You can also simply dip your fingers into the wash and

anoint the sachet. Keep the sachet with you until you have the sex life that you desire. Dispose of the contents appropriately.

Money & Luck

You can make charms for employment, general money, and luck, and the following spells are all works that relate to money or luck in some way. Of course, no magic will ever replace the value of earning your money.

FINANCIAL STABILITY CHARM

This charm protects you from sudden income changes or loss of money. Keep it by your primary door, or the door you most often use to enter your house, for best results.

MATERIALS
- Pen
- Paper
- 6-by-6-inch piece of green fabric
- 2 2-foot pieces of green thread
- Sewing needle
- 1 silver dollar (for prosperity)
- 2 tablespoons ground cinnamon or 1 cinnamon stick cut in half (for money, wealth)
- 1 vanilla bean or 3 tablespoons vanilla extract (for wealth)
- 5 tablespoons dried yellow or orange marigold petals (for protection of money)

WORKING

1. Use the pen to write out how much money you need each month to be comfortable on the piece of paper. Include what you spend on bills and entertainment and what you need to save.

2. Fold the fabric in half toward you. Thread the needle with one piece of thread, and stitch up the sides of the fabric, as described in the basic sachet instructions. As you stitch, recite the following chant until both sides are finished:

   I have all the money I need. From financial stress I am freed.

3. Add the petition to the sachet.

4. Begin adding the other materials to the bag. As you add each item, state what it is being used for:

   Silver dollar, bring to me financial prosperity.

   Cinnamon, which is spicy, brings me money.

   Vanilla bean, sweet and old, brings us new gold.

   Marigold, yellow and bright, protects our money tonight.

5. Use the second piece of thread to tightly tie the bag shut.

6. Use your fingers to play with the closed bag to mix the ingredients. As you mix the bag, recite the following chant five times:

   I have all the money I need. From financial stress I am freed.

7. Keep the charm by the door you most often use to enter your house. Every time the door is used, the charm is activated. Create a new charm every time you move.

GAMBLING LUCK SACHET

This charm increases your luck and is to be carried when you go out to gamble. It's the perfect charm for vacations that involve gambling and casinos.

MATERIALS
- Pen
- Paper
- 4-by-6-inch piece of yellow or gold fabric
- Sewing needle
- 2 2-foot pieces of silver, gold, or yellow thread
- 3 fool's gold tumbles (for luck)
- 3 alligator teeth (for gambling luck)
- Allspice kernel (to attract luck)
- Nutmeg seed (for luck)
- Rabbit's foot (to attract luck)

WORKING
1. Use the pen to write out "Good luck today as I gamble and play." on the paper.

2. Fold the fabric in half toward you. Thread the needle with one strand of thread, and sew up the two sides, as described in the basic sachet instructions. As you sew up the sachet, chant:

> *Lady Luck come today. By my side you*
> *shall stay while games of luck I do play.*

3. Add all of the materials except for the petition. As you add each item, state why it is being used.

4. Recite your petition over the sachet like a prayer, and place the petition paper into the sachet.

5. Use the second thread and tie the sachet shut.

6. Play with the sachet for a few minutes, reciting the chant used while sewing five to seven times.

7. Carry the sachet with you whenever you are gambling. Store the sachet when not in use. Before you use the sachet again, feed it with oil or incense. Dispose of the materials when you get rid of the charm.

JOB-SEEKING SACHET

I have used this sachet many times, and each time, the sachet became more effective. Sleep with this charm under your pillow nightly until you are employed. Carry it with you when going to an interview. If you do this spell for someone else, remember to first get their consent.

MATERIALS
- Pen
- 2 pieces of paper
- Homemade or store-bought yellow or gold sachet
- Personal effects such as hair, nails, and teeth (Photos and scraps of old clothes are good substitutes.)

- 1 tablespoon alfalfa (to attract money)
- 1 tablespoon dried yellow marigold petals (for protection of money)
- ¼ tablespoon ground nutmeg (for luck, prosperity)
- Small iron pyrite tumble (for money, luck)
- Small citrine tumble (for money, luck)

WORKING

1. Use the pen and paper to draft a petition for the job you want. Include salary, benefits, work environment, commute, etc. Write the final petition on the second piece of paper. Fold the finished petition, and place it into the sachet.

2. Place the personal effects into the sachet. Know that the magic will target and help you.

3. Add each of the remaining items to the sachet, stating why you are adding them. Feel their power flowing through the charm and around the sachet.

4. Close the sachet tight once everything is in it, and use your hands to play with the contents to mix the materials. As you play with the sachet, see yourself in your dream job and doing the job well. Hold the image as long as you can, releasing the image into the sachet when you can't hold it any longer. While playing with the sachet, recite this chant three to five times:

    A job that's new. A dream come true.

5. Place your sachet under your pillow. Sleep with it nightly. Before going to bed each night, work

the sachet while holding an image of you in your dream job. Next time you have an interview for this job or position, carry the sachet with you. During the 5 to 10 minutes before the interview, work the sachet and recite the same chant from step 4 five times.

6. When you have secured your dream job and been there for a month, remove the crystals from the sachet. Dispose of the herbal materials away from your home.

Protection Sachet Charms

Protection sachets make wonderful gifts to loved ones. These protection sachets offer an energetic boost that allows the subconscious to find ways to protect us.

OUT AND ABOUT PROTECTION SACHET

This sachet is a personal protection charm. Carry it with you for both physical and spiritual protection.

MATERIALS
- Homemade or store-bought black sachet
- Personal effects such as hair, nails, and teeth (for direct energetic connection and to act as an energetic decoy)
- Pen
- Paper
- 5 nails (for protection)

- 2 snowflake obsidian tumbles (for protection)
- 2 red jasper tumbles (for protection)
- Tiger's-eye tumble (for fierceness of a tiger, protection)
- 4 pieces devil's shoestring (for protection against evil)

WORKING

1. Hold the sachet and fill it with protective energy by reciting any protection prayers or mantras you may normally work with.

2. Use the pen to write your name on the paper. Under your name, write "Protection." Draw a shield around the words. Fold the paper in half and place it in the sachet.

3. Give your personal effect life, as described in part 1. Place the effect in the sachet, stating:

   Effect of mine, you shall be my decoy, taking attacks for me.

4. Place the nails in the sachet, stating:

   To protect and defend from any energetic attack.

5. Add the crystals to the sachet. As you add each crystal, feel a protective barrier being built around you that comes from the sachet. State that each crystal is being used for its unique protective qualities.

6. Add the devil's shoestring to the sachet. Visualize all negativity sent your way becoming entangled

within the devil's shoestring. When all of the devil's shoestring has been added, state:

> *To trip up all that would cause me harm.*

7. Pull the sachet closed, and swing the sachet by the drawstring or thread to charge it with power. As you swing the sachet, feel a protective barrier forming around you.

8. Carry the sachet with you at all times. When you are alone, work the sachet and feel its power flow through you, creating that energetic barrier. Know that you are protected from any harm.

FAMILY MEMBER PROTECTION SACHET

This charm bag is used to protect a family member outside their home. This charm protects them from any problems or issues they may encounter while living their life. Always create this sachet with the consent of the target.

MATERIALS
- 6-by-6-inch piece of your family member's old clothing or black fabric
- 2 2-foot pieces of black thread
- Sewing needle
- 2 pieces of paper
- Pen
- 4 pieces devil's shoestring (to repel negativity)
- Iron nail (for protection)

- 2 tablespoons ground angelica root (to ward against evil)
- Snowflake obsidian tumble (to neutralize negativity)

WORKING

1. Fold the fabric in half toward you. Thread the needle with one of the threads, and stitch the sides of the fabric to create that pouch. As you sew up the sides, recite Psalm 91:9–16:

> *Because you have made the Lord, who is*
> *my refuge,*
> *Even the Most High, your dwelling place,*
>
> *No evil shall befall you,*
> *Nor shall any plague come near your*
> *dwelling;*
>
> *For He shall give His angels charge over you,*
> *To keep you in all your ways.*
>
> *In their hands they shall bear you up,*
> *Lest you dash your foot against a stone.*
>
> *You shall tread upon the lion and the cobra,*
> *The young lion and the serpent you shall*
> *trample underfoot.*
>
> *"Because he has set his love upon Me, therefore*
> *I will deliver him;*
> *I will set him on high, because he has known*
> *My name.*
> *   He shall call upon Me, and I will answer*
> *him;*
> *I will be with him in trouble;*
> *I will deliver him and honor him.*
> *   With long life I will satisfy him,*
> *And show him My salvation."*

2. Use the pen to draft your petition to protect your loved one on the paper. Write your final petition on the second piece of paper. Fold the paper in half and place it in the pouch, stating:

   To protect (target's name).

3. Add the devil's shoestring, stating:

   To trip up all that would cause them harm.

4. Add the nail to the sachet with the statement:

   To protect today from ill will sent their way.

5. Sprinkle the angelica root into the sachet. As you sprinkle the root, state:

   Protection from above is sent with their love.

6. Add the snowflake obsidian. As you add the stone, say:

   Protect them for me. From negativity they are free.

7. Use the second thread to tie the sachet shut. Once the sachet is shut, hold the sachet in your hands and play with it. While you use your fingers to play with the bag, recite the psalm verses three times.

8. Give the bag to the person it is designed to protect. Have them carry it with them whenever they leave their home.

NIGHTMARE PROTECTION SACHET

This charm is created to ensure that a child sleeps well. The goal of this spell is to neutralize any external forces that may be causing nightmares and provide a peaceful night of sleep.

MATERIALS
- Paper
- Pen
- 6-by-6-inch piece of blue or purple fabric
- Sewing needle
- 2 2-foot pieces of silver thread
- 3 amethyst tumbles (for peaceful dreams and to protect sleep)
- 2 labradorite tumbles (for better dreams)
- Moonstone tumble (for dreams, peaceful sleep, tension release)
- 2 tablespoons dried chamomile (for dreams, protection, sleep)
- 2 tablespoons dried lavender (for dreams, protection, sleep, tension release)

WORKING
1. Use the pen to write out the name of the person you wish to have sweet dreams on the paper. Under their name write "Peaceful Sleep," "Beautiful Dreams," and "Protection from Nightmares." As you write those words, visualize your target sleeping peacefully without any type of nightmare.

2. Fold the fabric in half toward you. Thread the needle with one strand of thread, and stitch up the sides of the fabric, as described in the basic sachet instructions. Recite the following chant until both sides are stitched:

   Sleep peacefully. Dream beautifully.

3. Place the petition in the sachet.

4. Add the amethyst crystals to the sachet. As you place them in the sachet, state:

   For peaceful sleep and beautiful dreams.

5. Add the labradorite crystals. As you add the them, state:

   For the ease of better dreams.

6. Place the moonstone in the sachet, stating:

   To release tension and bring peaceful dreams.

7. Add the herbs to the sachet. As you add them, state:

   To protect against bad dreams; to bring peaceful sleep.

8. Take the other thread and tie the sachet shut. Hold the sachet in your hands. As you hold the sachet, sing a portion of Johannes Brahms's "Wiegenlied" or a lullaby of your choice five to seven times:

   Lullaby and goodnight,
   With roses bestride
   With lilies bedecked, 'neath baby's sweet bed

*May thou sleep, may thou rest, may thy
slumber be blest*

*May thou sleep, may thou rest, may thy
slumber be blest.*

9. Place the sachet under the child's pillowcase.
   Once a week, remove the charm to work it. Use
   the charm for as long as necessary. Dispose of
   the sachet when the nightmares pass.

Psychic Development Charms

Psychic development is a part of learning to work and practice
magic. These charms are useful aids to enhance your work. To
have strong psychic senses you must put in the work. No spell
or charm will grant you psychic talents.

PSYCHIC DREAMS SACHET

Use this charm to have lucid dreams or dreams with
psychic messages. This charm can be used in addition to other psychic development charms for best
results.

You can find the recipes for the psychic development incense and psychic development oil in part 3.

MATERIALS
- 3-by-6-inch piece of purple fabric
- Sewing needle
- 6 inches of purple thread
- Pin

- Purple candle
- Psychic development incense
- Charcoal disc and censer/incense burner
- Matches or lighter
- Psychic development oil
- Opalite tumble (for abilities, psychic gifts)
- 2 tablespoons dried mugwort (for psychic development, psychic powers)
- 1 tablespoon dried lavender (for mental focus)
- 1 tablespoon dried yellow marigold petals (for opening psychic sight)
- 2 amethyst tumbles (for psychic abilities)
- 1 tablespoon dried rosemary (for memory)
- 5 drops rosemary essential oil (for memory)
- 6 to 8 inches of silver thread

WORKING

1. Fold the fabric in half. Thread the needle with the purple thread and stitch the sides, as described in the basic sachet instructions. Chant as you sew:

   Open my third eye tonight. My dreams activate psychic sight.

2. Use the pin to carve something like "Increase Psychic Skills" into the candle.

3. Place the incense in the censer or burner. Use the matches or lighter to light the incense and candle.

4. Pass each of the remaining materials except the oil and thread through the incense smoke and

over the candle flame. Then add each component to the sachet, stating their use:

> *Opalite, strengthen psychic sight.*
>
> *Mugwort, witches' herb, enhances psychic senses tonight.*
>
> *Lavender for sleep at night, for dreams enhance psychic might.*
>
> *Marigold, yellow and bright, lights the way to the third eye this day.*
>
> *Amethyst, purple and clear, provides protection clearing fear.*
>
> *Rosemary that I may remember my dreams and all messages within.*

5. Use the silver thread to tie the bag shut.

6. Anoint the bag with the rosemary oil. Hold the bag in your hands and play with it until you feel the materials are well mixed. Extinguish the incense and candle.

7. Place the sachet under your pillow. Record any dreams that you remember each morning. Take special notice of any recurring themes, symbols, or people. These recurring items could be clues to a message that a spirit is trying to give you. Feed the bag with the rosemary oil once a week.

ENHANCE DIVINATION SACHET

This spell for divination is to enhance your skills. Store the sachet with your divination tools. Hold the sachet in your lap when doing readings.

MATERIALS
- 4-by-4-inch piece of purple fabric
- 2 8-inch pieces of purple or silver thread
- Sewing needle
- Personal effect such as a lock of hair, tooth, or fingernail (A photo or scrap of old clothing is a good substitute.)
- 1 tablespoon dried eyebright (for psychic senses)
- 1 tablespoon dried goldenrod (for divination)
- 1 teaspoon dried arnica flowers (for psychic powers)
- Celestite tumble (to stimulate psychic abilities)
- Fluorite tumble (for mental clarity)

WORKING
1. Fold the fabric in half. Thread the needle with one piece of thread, and stitch a basic sachet, sewing the two sides and leaving the top open. As you sew the bag, chant:

    Psychic sight open tonight. Provide true and accurate insight.

2. Place your personal effect into the sachet.

3. Add the herbs to the sachet. As you add them, state:

    Herbs of psychic sight, lend me your power tonight.

4. Place the crystals in the sachet. As you add each one, state:

   Crystal of the mind, empower the herbs in kind.

5. Close the sachet with the remaining string. Hold the sachet to your third eye, and know your psychic senses have awakened. Keep the sachet at your third eye until you can no longer feel power radiating from the sachet. Once a week, hold the sachet to your third eye to strengthen your third eye.

6. Before you do any readings, hold the sachet to your third eye. When you can no longer sense the connection place the sachet in your lap.

7. When you are confident in your abilities, empty the sachet. The herbs can be used as a divination incense and the crystals as psychic charms.

Healing Sachets

The following sachets are charms related to healing. These charms cover mental health issues as well as physical ailments. No healing charm is a substitute for medical assistance. Always seek professional medical advice before working any sort of magic or natural charm.

ANXIETY EASE SACHET

This charm is used when stress or anxiety is over-whelming. It works best when carried with you. This is not a treatment for an anxiety disorder. For an anxiety disorder, seek professional treatment.

MATERIALS

- Rose and lavender incense (for peace, relaxation)
- Charcoal disc and censer/incense burner
- Matches or lighter
- 4-by-2-inch piece of blue fabric
- 2 6-inch pieces of blue thread
- Sewing needle
- 2 tablespoons dried lavender (for anxiety relief, peace)
- 1 tablespoon dried spearmint leaves (for peace, relaxation)
- 1 tablespoon dried chamomile (for anxiety relief)
- Amethyst tumble (for anxiety relief)
- Lepidolite tumble (for stress relief)
- Lavender essential oil, optional (for anxiety, stress relief and to feed the sachet)

WORKING

1. Calm your mind and body. Then use the matches or lighter to light your rose and lavender incense, placing it in your burner of choice.

2. Fold the fabric in half away from you. Thread the needle with one of the pieces of thread and stitch up the bag, sewing the two sides and leaving the

top open. As you stitch up the bag, recite this chant three to five times:

To relieve anxiety; from anxiety I am free.

3. Add the other materials except the remaining thread and oil to the bag. As you add each item, state what their jobs are:

Lavender for anxiety relief and peace of mind.

Spearmint to calm and relax me.

Chamomile for anxiety relief and peace of spirit.

Amethyst for stress release.

Lepidolite to ease anxiety.

4. Take the remaining thread and tie the sachet shut. Pass the sachet through the incense smoke, reciting the following chant five times:

Anxiety, from you I am free.

5. Extinguish the incense.

6. Keep the charm with you at all times. When you have a higher sense of anxiety than normal, work the bag for a few minutes. As you work the bag, recite the chant from step 4 five to seven times.

7. Feed the sachet weekly by passing it through the incense smoke. If you have lavender essential oil, you can use that instead of the incense.

STOMACH RELIEF SACHET

This sachet is designed to help deal with intestinal distress. This spell relies on both the medicinal and magical properties of the contents. This spell is for times when you would use things like mint tea or an antacid to settle your stomach. If the distress persists more than four days or gets worse, seek medical attention. Refill the sachet each time you need to use it.

MATERIALS
- Homemade or store-bought blue sachet
- 1 tablespoon dried angelica leaves (for indigestion relief)
- 1 tablespoon dried catnip (for indigestion relief, peace, relaxation)
- 1 tablespoon ground ginger (for protection from stomachaches, stomach relief)
- 1 tablespoon dried spearmint leaves (for calm, indigestion relief, peace, stress relief, tranquility)
- Peppermint essential oil (for indigestion relief, relaxation, stress relief)
- Chamomile essential oil (for indigestion relief, peace, relaxation, tranquility)

WORKING
1. Fill the sachet with the herbs. As you add each herb, state what work they have ahead of them.

2. Close the sachet, then cover it with the essential oils. As you rub the oils over the sachet, let their scents heal you.

3. Once the sachet is covered with the oils, hold it tight. As you hold the sachet, see a blue healing light flowing from and surrounding the sachet. While watching the light grow, state this chant five times:

Light of blue, healing renew.

4. Place the charged sachet against your stomach under your clothes. Keep the sachet there until your intestinal distress goes away. For the next week, feed the sachet peppermint essential oil daily. At the end of the week, toss the herbs away and wash the sachet.

Miscellaneous Sachets

The last two sachets I have for you are oddballs; they don't fit into any of the other categories. I thought these were fun spells, and I think you will enjoy them too.

STUDY AID SACHET

This spell is a variation on a sachet that I have made for myself. The goal of this sachet is to enhance your memory and open mental clarity. This does not replace studying, but it does boost the results of it.

MATERIALS
- Homemade or store-bought blue sachet
- 1 teaspoon dried rosemary (for memory)
- 1 teaspoon dried ginkgo leaves (for mental focus)
- 1 teaspoon dried lavender (for mental abilities, peace)
- Agate tumble (for mental clarity)
- Fluorite tumble (for clarity of thought)
- Rose quartz tumble (for confidence, self-love)

WORKING
1. Sprinkle the rosemary into the sachet, stating:

   I call upon rosemary to strengthen my memory.

2. Sprinkle the ginkgo leaves into the sachet. As you sprinkle them, state:

   Ginkgo leaf, I call upon thee to help me think clearly.

3. Add the lavender. As you add the herb, say:

   Lavender, I call upon you to provide a peace strong and true.

4. Add the crystals, stating why you are working with them. Feel their power add to the sachet.

5. Seal the sachet. Hold it in your hands and play with it. As you play with the sachet, focus on doing well in your studies.

6. Hold the sachet to your forehead for 5 minutes. Feel the energy from the sachet enter your mind and energize your brain. Know that you will have a greater understanding of your subject matter.

7. Before you do any homework, hold the sachet to your forehead, and feel the power of the sachet flowing into your mind, providing focus and clarity. Hold the sachet during homework and studying. Work the sachet before any exams.

SAINT PETER OPEN OPPORTUNITIES SACHET

Keys are one of the symbols of Saint Peter, and this sachet calls on his power to unlock the paths before you. Use this spell to open opportunities in your future.

MATERIALS
- Homemade or store-bought yellow sachet
- 1 tablespoon dried lemon balm (to open roads)
- 1 tablespoon dried basil (to clear blocks, open roads)
- 1 teaspoon dried rosemary leaves (to clear blocks, open roads)
- 1 pinch crossroads dirt (to connect to paths and roads, symbolize Saint Peter)
- 1 skeleton key, which can be found at a hardware store, or a key without a lock (to open locked doors, symbolize Saint Peter)

WORKING
1. Hold the sachet to your heart for 5 minutes. As you hold the sachet, visualize a closed and locked gate unlocking and opening for you. Direct the energy of that image into the sachet.

2. Begin to add the herbs. As you add each herb, state why you are using it. Feel the herbs clearing any blocks in your way. Direct that energy into the sachet.

3. Sprinkle the crossroads dirt into the sachet. As you sprinkle dirt, recite the following statement:

   Saint Peter, holder of heaven's keys, I ask you to open the doors for me that my dream may become reality.

4. Add the skeleton key to the sachet. As you place the skeleton key in the sachet, visualize all potential paths before you open. Direct that energy into the sachet.

5. Close and begin to play with the sachet. Feel any doors that were in your way suddenly spring open. As you play with the sachet, recite the following Saint Peter Prayer five to seven times:

   O God, who hast given unto Thy blessed Apostle Peter the keys to thy kingdom of heaven, and the power to bind and loose: grant that we may be delivered, through the help of his intercession, from the slavery to all our sins: Who livest and reignest world without end.[5]

6. Carry the sachet with you for as long as you feel the need to ensure that all blocks in your path are gone. Recharge the sachet once a week by

---

5. Catholic Online, "St. Peter."

working the sachet and reciting the Saint Peter Prayer five times.

7. When you no longer feel the need to carry the sachet and want to end the charm, bury the herbs at a crossroads near you with a thank you to Saint Peter. Cleanse the crystals as your intuition dictates.

PACKET SPELLS

Packet magic is not a common form of container magic. However, it is the easiest to work. With packet magic, you are creating the container from often unusual materials. Packet spells are designed for quick, fast results. You work packets until the goal manifests, then destroy the packet to end the magical work. The spirit can be absorbed back into nature.

Creating the Packets

Packets are able to work magic using just the power within the petition. The petitions are filled with intense mental and emotional energy. That energy provides the initial energetic charge. Herbs and roots are occasionally added for extra power. Power is then raised and released through the process of creating and sealing the container.

To add herbs, roots, dirt, and other materials to a paper packet, sprinkle or place the materials over your petition. After these materials have been added to the petition, you can begin to fold your packet. While the paper is being folded, mantras, chants, or affirmations are recited. The words charge the packet while the folding raises and seals in energy. These packets are then wrapped with ribbon or cord to seal in the energy.

Fabric packets are made by stitching fabric around the petition or curios. The fabric color should correspond to the magical goal. Each stitch adds power and energy to the work. Like with paper packets, mantras, chants, or affirmations are recited as these packets are stitched together.

Empowering Paper Packets

Intent and sigils provide the base charge for your paper packets. The remaining power needed comes from the sealing of the packets. For paper packets, how you fold the material is important. If you are attracting something, fold the material toward you. To remove something from your life, fold away from you. Both ways of folding show the energy what you want done.

One of the ways that I make sure the materials are folded evenly is rotating the materials 90 degrees after each fold.

You either turn the packet 90 degrees toward you (bringing to you) or away from you (removal). The rotating ensures that the paper packets are folded evenly and that the power is distributed through the packet as it is worked and created.

The chants and mantras recited while folding the paper are the final ingredient for effective packet magic. Words evoke emotions, physical reactions, and mental images. As you speak the words, direct their energy into the folds. Each fold seals in the energy from the chants, intent, and the fold, and the folding of the material creates the packets. Once you're done folding the packets, it's time to seal them.

Sealing Packets and Witches' Ladders

Wrapping the folded or stuffed container with ribbon or thread is one of the ways these containers can be sealed. When you wrap the packets with the ribbon, you seal in the energy from folding and pounding the materials. While you wrap the packet, recite the same chants or mantras you recited while folding it.

Make sure the entire packet is covered with the ribbon. The packet will get wrapped in multiple layers of ribbon. When one layer of ribbon is completed, rotate the packet like when you folded the paper. After rotating the packet, tie a knot, sealing in the energy of the packet. In some spells, you may choose to continue knotting, using something called a witches' ladder.

WITCHES' LADDER CHARM

Witches' ladders are their own powerful form of spellwork and are used in many types of spells. Including witches' ladders in your packet magic adds another layer of spell crafting to your magic. Witches' ladders are a series of nine to ten knots tied to raise energy and seal magic at the same time. Traditionally, the charm goes like this, with a knot tied with each line:

By knot of one, the spell has begun.

By knot of two, this spell is new.

By knot of three, this spell is for me.

By knot of four, magic is in store.

By knot of five, this spell is alive.

By knot of six, this spell I do fix.

By knot of seven, this spell reaches heaven.

By knot of eight, this magic becomes fate.

By knot of nine, my desires are mine.

By knot of ten, the magic begins again.

As you tie each knot, direct your intent into the ribbon. Your intent is all you need to power the witches' ladder. Each knot adds and seals the energy of the witches' ladder to the packet. The energy raised from your focused intent and the tying of the knots remains sealed until the knots are untied or cut.

The chant can be altered for when stitches are used. Instead of tying a knot, make your stitch, and replace the word *knot* with *stitch* in the charm. After ten stitches, start the chant again and repeat until the container is fully stitched. Just direct your intent through the stitch, and you can work a witches' ladder through stitches.

Paper Packet Spells

Paper packets are my favorite type of packet spell. I first learned this form of magic when I was living in a group home. I was unable to burn candles or incense and had very little storage space. My appreciation for paper packets began there.

EMPOWER YOUR DIVINATION TOOL

The goal of this spell is to empower you and increase your connection to your divination tool. Store the packet with your divination tool.

MATERIALS
- 2 pieces of paper
- Purple pen
- 2 dried bay leaves (for divination, psychic powers)
- 1 teaspoon dried goldenrod (for divination)
- Sprig of fresh rosemary (for concentration, mental focus, mind)
- 2 feet of silver ribbon

WORKING

1. Use your pen to write out your intent on one piece of paper. Follow the steps from part 1 to create a sigil. On the second slip of paper, rewrite your petition. Under the petition, draw an eye with your sigil in the center.

2. On the first bay leaf, write "Empower Divination." On the second bay leaf, write "Awakened Psychic Senses." Place the bay leaves on top of the petition.

3. Sprinkle the goldenrod over the bay leaves. As you sprinkle the goldenrod, state:

   Goldenrod, yellow and bright, empower my divination on this night.

4. Place the rosemary over the other herbs. As you place the sprig, state:

   Herb of the mind, grant me the power to divine.

5. Fold the paper in half toward you, stating:

   Clear psychic sight, accurate divination each night.

6. Rotate the paper packet 90 degrees toward you, fold the paper, and repeat the chant from step 5. Repeat the process three to five times after the first two folds.

7. Tie the ribbon around the packet, and wrap the packet with the ribbon, bringing the ribbon toward yourself. After five wraps, tie the first

knot in your witches' ladder. Rotate the packet
90 degrees toward you. Repeat until the witches'
ladder is complete.

8. Once the ladder has been finished, place the
packet with your preferred divination tool.
Thirty minutes before your next divination ses-
sion, hold the packet to your forehead. Visualize
purple light flowing from the packet into your
forehead. Hold the packet in one hand while
doing the reading.

9. Burn the packet when you no longer need the extra
boost. Make a packet for each divination tool.

SPIRIT BLESSING PACKET

Use this packet to carry the blessings of a specific
spirit. Charge this packet during any working dedicated to the spirit. Ask for the spirit's consent first.

MATERIALS
- Frankincense and copal incense (to attract and
  honor spirits)
- Charcoal disc and censer/incense burner
- Matches or lighter
- Gold or silver pen
- Paper
- 1 tablespoon dried angelica root (to attract spirits)
- 1 tablespoon dragon's blood resin (for dragon
  spirits)
- 1 tablespoon myrrh resin (to attract spirits)
- 1 foot of white ribbon

WORKING

1. Use the matches or lighter to light the incense and invite your spirit guide into your workspace.

2. Use the pen to write the name of the spirit whose blessings you want to carry on the paper. Under their name, write "Blessings."

3. Pass the paper through the incense smoke five times, stating:

   I feel the spirit's power, lending me their blessings this hour.

4. Pass the herbs through the incense smoke five times, stating:

   Spirit power, bless me this hour.

5. Sprinkle all the herbs over the written words.

6. Fold the packet toward you, stating:

   Blessings called today, with me stay.

7. Rotate the paper 90 degrees toward you. Fold the paper and repeat the statement from step 5. Repeat the process five to seven times.

8. Tie a knot around the packet with the ribbon, and wrap the packet, bringing the ribbon toward you. When the packet is covered in ribbon, tie another knot in the ribbon. After the knot is tied, pass the packet through the incense smoke five times, stating:

   Blessings today, in this packet stay.

9. Extinguish the incense.

10. Carry the packet with you to feel the blessings of your spirit ally. To recharge the packet, once a month pass the packet through incense smoke given as an offering to the spirit.

STRENGTH & COURAGE PACKET

This spell can be used anytime you need that extra courage to get through the day.

MATERIALS
- Pen
- 2 pieces of paper
- 1 teaspoon frankincense resin (for inner strength, protection)
- 1 teaspoon dried woodruff (for courage, strength)
- 1 teaspoon dried plantain (for strength)
- 1 teaspoon myrrh resin (for inner strength, protection)
- 1 foot of yellow or orange ribbon

WORKING
1. Use the pen to write out why you need the boost in courage on the paper. See yourself having the courage you need. If necessary, write a clean version of the petition on the second piece of paper.

2. Sprinkle the herbs over the paper, stating:

   For strength and courage.

3. Fold the paper in half toward you and repeat the same mantra from step 2. Rotate the paper 90

degrees toward you, repeating the fold, mantra, and rotate process three to five times.

4. Using the ribbon, tie a knot around the packet. Wrap the packet, bringing the ribbon toward you as you wrap. Once the packet is covered, begin your witches' ladder.

5. Carry the packet with you. Before you face a problem or need courage, work the packet three times, reciting your mantra. When you no longer need the boost in courage, dispose of the packet via burning or throwing it in the trash.

FIND AN APARTMENT PACKET

I wrote this spell for the first apartment my husband and I shared. As I wrote the spell, I made sure everything we needed was included in the petition. We got the first apartment we looked at.

MATERIALS
- Green pen
- 2 pieces of paper
- Sprig of fresh rosemary (for home and house blessings)
- 1 teaspoon fresh or dried basil (for house blessings)
- 1 foot of green ribbon
- Fire extinguisher or large container full of water
- Matches or lighter

WORKING

1. Use the pen to draft your petition on one piece of paper. Include details like rent, location, accessibility, etc. On the same piece of paper, draw a potential floor plan. See yourself living there happily. Draw the final petition and floor plan on the second piece of paper.

2. Place the rosemary and basil across the petition. State:

   For home blessings.

3. Put the paper with the floor plan on top of the herbs with the floor plan facing the herbs. Fold the papers in half toward you. As you fold the paper, state:

   A new home for me to live independently.

4. Rotate the paper 90 degrees toward you. Repeat the fold and statement three to five times.

5. Once you have a small bundle, make your first wrap around the packet with the ribbon. Tie a knot to secure the ribbon. Wrap the packet with the ribbon, reciting the mantra from step 3. After five wraps of the ribbon, tie a knot to begin the witches' ladder.

6. Rotate the packet 90 degrees toward you and start wrapping the packet again. Repeat the process until the witches' ladder is complete. Tie one last knot, stating:

   The spell is cast; my desire comes to pass.

7. Carry the packet with you every day while you are apartment searching. When you see an apartment, arrive slightly early to the showing and work the packet three times, using the same mantra as before.

8. When you have secured your home, prepare your outdoor workspace to burn the packet, bringing a fire extinguisher or water with just in case. Use the matches or lighter to set the packet on fire. Once the fire has burned out and the ashes are cool, stomp down on the ashes. Scatter the ashes around the property. Thank the land spirit for letting you live there.

STRENGTHEN OUR LOVE PACKET

This spell is for when you and your partner are going through a difficult time. The goal is to keep your connection strong enough to work through your situation. This spell worked for me, and I hope it works for you too.

MATERIALS
- Red pen
- Paper
- Handful of fresh red rose petals (for love)
- Handful of fresh lavender flowers (for love)
- 3 feet of red ribbon
- Scissors or knife

WORKING

1. Use the pen to write the names of you and your partner. Under the names, write "Strengthen Our Connection." Direct the energy of your love into the words you write.

2. Sprinkle the flowers over the writing, stating:

   For a love that's strong, that will last a while long.

3. Fold the paper in half toward you. As you fold the paper toward you, state:

   A love that's strong, doing well, getting along.

4. Rotate the paper 90 degrees toward you. Fold the paper in half again, repeating your chant three to five times. Fold the paper in half again, repeating the chant.

5. Tie a knot around the packet with the ribbon, and wrap it with the ribbon. As you wrap the package, chant:

   Two hearts now bound; true love be found.

6. Wrap the packet until it's covered. Rotate the packet 90 degrees. Repeat three times.

7. Either tie a final knot around the packet and seal in the energy you have raised, or continue to empower your packet by creating a witches' ladder.

8. Carry the package with you every day. As long as you carry this package, your love will be strong.

Once you feel the relationship is stable again, cut the ribbon. As you cut the ribbon, state:

> *From this bind we are free, lest our love be true naturally.*

9. After the ribbon has been cut, toss the packet in a trash can away from your home.

To Cause Someone to Lose Their Way

The goal of this spell is to cause your target to forget about you and go back to their own life. Use this spell when your target has been cutting corners or spreading lies.

When gathering the fire ants used in this spell, be sure to use gloves, only collecting ants that are already dead.

MATERIALS
- Pen
- Slip of paper
- Unsolved maze puzzle printed on fresh, clean paper
- 3 crushed fire ants (for confusion)
- 1 crushed snail shell (to delay, slow down, stall)
- 1 teaspoon poppy seeds (for confusion)
- 1 foot of silver or metallic ribbon

WORKING
1. On the slip of paper, use the pen to write your target's name. Tear the name from the paper. Put the name in the center of the maze.

2. Sprinkle the remaining materials except the ribbon over the maze. Fold the paper in half away from you, stating:

   To lose your way, in this maze shall you stay.

3. Rotate the packet 90 degrees away from you and repeat the fold and statement. Do this three to five times.

4. Tie a knot around the packet using the ribbon. Then wrap the packet with the ribbon, wrapping away from you. As you wrap the packet, state:

   By this thread I do bind; an exit you will never find.

5. When you feel that the packet has been wrapped enough, bring the packet where your target will pass it during their daily life.

6. When your target has learned their lesson, destroy the packet and toss it into a trash can away from your target.

Fabric Packets

The difference between a packet and a sachet is that packets are sewn shut and sachets are not. Sachets have an opening that is tied shut. They are reusable. Packets, however, are sewn completely shut and then disposed of when the spell has manifested. Packets are a one-time spell charm.

CHEER UP PACKET

This spell is based on a charm my husband created for me. Whenever I held the piece of fabric, I would cheer up and feel better.

MATERIALS

- Pen
- Paper
- Scissors
- 4-by-4-inch piece of yellow fabric
- 1 teaspoon fresh or dried sunflower petals (for happiness, joy)
- 1 teaspoon fresh or dried catnip (for happiness, joy)
- 1 teaspoon fresh or dried mullein (for courage, strength)
- Sewing needle
- 12 to 18 inches of yellow, gold, or orange thread

WORKING

1. Use the pen to write "Happiness," "Inner Strength," "Joy," and "Love" on the paper. Write each word under the other.

2. Use the scissors to cut the paper, leaving each of the words on its own small slip. Place the slips on the square of fabric.

3. Sprinkle the herbs over the slips of paper. As you sprinkle the herbs, direct the energy of love and joy into them.

4. Fold the fabric over the herbs and paper. Thread the needle with the thread, and stitch up the packet. As you stitch the packet, chant:

   Love, peace, and happiness.

5. Place the packet somewhere so you can carry it with you daily, such as a purse or bag. Whenever you doubt yourself or feel down, hold the packet to your heart. Let the emotions from the packet flow into you. Hold the packet as long as you need to.

6. When the packet falls apart, thank the packet, and toss it away. You no longer need its power.

CURSE-BREAKING PACKET

Use this packet spell to cleanse yourself when you feel you have been cursed.

MATERIALS
- White washcloth
- 6 dried bay leaves (to remove evil)
- 3 pieces of birch bark (for purification)
- Zest of 1 lemon (to clear and cut negativity and evil)
- 1 tablespoon dried sage (to guard against the evil eye)
- 1 tablespoon dried woodruff (for overcoming adversaries)
- 12 to 18 inches of white or silver thread
- Sewing needle
- Bowl or wash basin
- Hot water

- 5 drops pine essential oil (for purification)
- Sprig of fresh rosemary (to repel evil)

WORKING

1. Place the white washcloth on your workspace. In the center of the washcloth, place 5 bay leaves, the birch bark, lemon zest, sage, and woodruff.

2. Thread the needle with the thread, and sew the packet closed. As you stitch, state:

   Evil and ill will caught today, I banish you away. Your curses shall not stay.

3. Fill the bowl or wash basin with water. Add the pine essential oil, remaining bay leaf, and sprig of rosemary. As you add these materials, feel the water being filled with a white, sacred light.

4. Swirl the packet in the bowl or basin of water. Once the packet is soaked, remove it from the water and squeeze out the excess liquid.

5. Use the packet to wipe yourself down from head to toe using downward motions. Soak the packet as needed to continue.

6. When your body has been fully wiped down, let the packet dry. Pour the water down the drain.

7. Dispose of the packet in the trash after use. Due to the possibility of mold, this packet needs to be remade every time you use the spell.

8. Repeat the spell weekly as needed.

STRENGTHEN MALE FERTILITY

This spell focuses on enhancing male fertility. If it is not done for you, only perform this spell with consent. A similar female fertility spell is included in the "Poppet & Doll Spells" chapter.

MATERIALS

- 2 4-by-4-inch pieces of you or your partner's old, clean underwear or green fabric
- 3 acorns (for male fertility)
- 3 moss agate tumbles (for fertility)
- Small mixing bowl and spoon or mortar and pestle
- 1 teaspoon dried catnip (for fertility)
- 1 teaspoon dried ginkgo leaves (for fertility)
- 1 teaspoon dried pine needles (for fertility)
- 1 teaspoon dried Saint-John's-wort (for strength)
- 1 foot of green thread
- Sewing needle

WORKING

1. Place the acorns and moss agate tumbles in a cross on top of one of the fabric squares. As you place these curios, state:

   For strong fertility.

2. Mix the remaining herbs in the bowl with the spoon or in the mortar with the pestle. As you mix and grind the herbs, focus on having a healthy and safe pregnancy. Direct that energy into the herbal mixture.

3. Pour the herb mixture over the cross. Cover as much of the cross as you can with the herbs.

4. Place the second fabric square over the first. Thread the needle with the thread, and stitch the packet closed. As you stitch the packet closed, chant:

   Pregnancy and fertility.

5. Place the packet under your mattress. Keep the packet there until the pregnancy ends.

Other Packets

Packets can also be made from other materials. These packet spells are unique. To make these packets, the petitions are encased in a container that is created as part of the spellcasting process.

SILVER DOLLAR MONEY PACKET

This spell comes from the superstition that an empty wallet invites financial distress. To prevent this distress, make sure you always have some form of currency in your wallet.

MATERIALS
- Five-dollar bill or paper bills of equal value (for money)
- Silver dollar or coins of equal value (for money)
- Dash of ground cinnamon (for money)
- Dash of ground cloves (for money, prosperity)

- Dash of ground allspice (for money, prosperity)
- 1 foot of green or gold ribbon

WORKING

1. Place the dollar bill face down with the coin in the center.

2. Sprinkle the spices over the coin.

3. Fold the bill over the coin until the coin is encased by the bill.

4. Wrap the currency packet with the ribbon until the packet is covered. As you wrap the packet, state:

   Packet of currency, protect my money.

5. Keep the packet in your wallet at all times. As long as you have this packet in your wallet, you will always have the money to be able to live happily.

SEASHELL CLEANSE PACKET

This is a cleansing spell that uses the power of the tides to remove things from your life. Anytime you are at an ocean beach, you can use this spell to cleanse yourself.

MATERIALS

- 2 mussel or clam shells of the same size
- 2 teaspoons salt (to absorb and neutralize negativity)
- 1 teaspoon crushed cedar greens (for purification)

- Crushed pine needle bough (for cleansing)
- Handful of beach sand

WORKING

1. In one of the shells, sprinkle the curios. As you add the curios, know they will remove the unwanted forces from your life. Place the other shell on top, completing your container.

2. Hold the shells together, and brush the shell over your body, starting at your crown and moving down to your feet.

3. When the tide changes from high to low, place the shell in sand near the water. Safely step on the shell and crush it, grinding the shell into as many pieces as you can. While crushing the shell, state:

   Salt and herbs by the sea, remove all negativity from me. From that force I wish to be free.

4. Walk away and let the waves wash the shell out to sea. Know that as the crushed shell is washed to sea, you will be free from unwanted influences in your life.

REFLECT & PROTECT MIRROR PACKET

Use this spell to return any negativity back to the sender and to protect yourself from any unwanted attention. If you have done anything to instigate the behavior, this spell will not work.

This spell can be modified to work as a protection charm that simply reflects attacks off you without necessarily targeting the sender. To modify the spell, replace the paper with a personal effect and change the word *return* to *reflect* in the charm.

MATERIALS
- Small dual-sided compact mirror
- Pen
- Small slip of paper
- 1 teaspoon ground dried galangal root (for justice work, protection and to return to sender)
- ¼ teaspoon ground cayenne pepper (for protection, removal)
- ¼ teaspoon ground black pepper
- 2 feet of black ribbon
- Scissors

WORKING
1. Use the pen to write "Return to Sender" and your target's name on both sides of the slip of paper. Place the paper in the center of the open compact.

2. Sprinkle the herbs over the paper and state:

   Return back all that is an attack.

3. Shut the compact. Use the ribbon to tie a knot around the compact, and wrap the ribbon around it three times, stating:

   Mirror compact reflect and protect.

4. Flip the compact over, and wrap it three more times, repeating the same chant from step 3.

Repeat the process of flipping, wrapping, and chanting five times.

5. Carry the charm with you in some fashion until you feel its power is no longer needed.

6. When you feel your target learned their lesson, cut the ribbon with scissors. Toss the paper and herbs into the trash. Cleanse the compact and go about your life.

To Shut Someone Up

This is a traditional Conjure trick to shut someone up or stop their actions. The packet, which is a beef tongue, is placed away from your home and where wild animals can get to it. As the animals eat the packet, the spell is released. When the tongue is gone, your target has learned their lesson. Since animals will eat this packet, be sure to use nontoxic ink and natural, biodegradable materials.

MATERIALS
- Pen
- Paper
- Knife
- Beef tongue (to represent speaking, the voice)
- 5 drops lemon juice (for hexing, reversal, souring)
- 1 tablespoon ground cayenne pepper (to cause pain in their mouths when gossiping)
- Sewing needle
- 1 to 2 feet of black upholstery thread

- Hammer
- Nail
- About 1 foot of natural rope or thread

WORKING

1. Use the pen to write out the name or names of the people you want to stop from gossiping on the paper. Tear each of the names from the paper.

2. Use the knife to slice open the beef tongue. Pull the cut apart to create an opening that you can stuff the paper and herbs into.

3. Insert the pieces of paper into the tongue, spitting on each name as you stuff it in.

4. Squeeze the lemon juice over the names, then sprinkle the cayenne pepper on top.

5. Using the needle and thread, sew up the tongue, leaving the names inside.

6. Take the beef tongue, hammer, nail, and the rope out into the woods, and hammer the tongue into a tree. Use the rope to tie the tongue to the tree trunk, securing it in a second way. Walk away knowing that animals with eat the tongue, releasing the spell, until it is gone. When the tongue is gone, your target has learned their lesson.

To Cause Bad Luck Packet

Use this packet to bring bad luck to an individual. This jinx will cause your target to have a series of misfortunes.

When gathering the fire ants used in this spell, be sure to use gloves, only collecting ants that are already dead.

MATERIALS
- Rabbit's foot key chain
- Knife
- 3 black cat whiskers (for bad luck)
- Small piece of black cat fur (for bad luck)
- Black cat claw (for bad luck)
- 3 crushed fire ants (for cursing)
- 5 drops lemon (for souring)
- Thread the same color as the rabbit's foot and twice its length
- Sewing needle

WORKING
1. Remove the chain and end cap from the rabbit's foot, and remove any fillings, focusing on your target and why you wish them ill. Direct that energy into the rabbit's foot.

2. Fill the hollow part of rabbit's foot with the black cat materials. As you add the curios, state:

   To bring bad luck.

3. Add the fire ants, stating:

   For chaos and confusion among the bad luck.

4. Squirt the juice over the materials. As you squirt the juice, state:

   To sour the luck sent your way.

5. Sew the opening you created closed, and add the key chain portion back on.

6. The next time you see your target, give them the rabbit's foot as a "peace offering." Walk away knowing they will have bad luck.

POPPET &
DOLL SPELLS

Poppets are a very old form of folk magic, and they are one of the most fictionalized and demonized magical practices. When people think of dolls and magic, they almost always think of curses, hexes, and all sorts of baneful magic. They think of the voodoo doll. Hollywood and other media did a really good job of taking a simple magical spell and turning it into something scary.

In spellwork, poppets are ideal to target specific individuals and work on people from a distance. These spells work by creating a human-shaped figure that is named after your target and filled with personal effects and curios. Whatever happens to the doll, happens to the target. The more personal effects that you incorporate, the stronger the connection to the target and the magic.

Poppet Magic Basics

There are some metaphysical, Conjure, and occult shops that sell ready-to-use poppet dolls. These kits come with specific intents, such as healing or hexing. All you need to do is fill the poppet and do the work.

If you are not crafty or creatively inclined, you can also work poppet magic by using toy dolls. Stuffed dolls can be gently cut open and filled with herbs and other materials related to the work at hand, but nearly any sort of doll can be worked with. You can even use plastic, solid-body dolls and action figures. When working with these types of poppets, remove the head of the figure and stuff the body with herbs and curios for the work. Another way to work with plastic dolls is using anointing oils and stuffing the clothing.

Unless you are working with pre-stuffed dolls, most of your poppets are not going to be very fluffy or full. That doesn't matter. As long as the fillings are mixed throughout the body, the magic will work. If you do want fluffy poppets, you can add fiberfill to your materials list. Add the fluffy filling between each curio you add.

Poppet Life

In order for poppet magic to work, the poppets must have life and energy. Many poppets fail to work because the practitioner forgot to give the poppet life. The following ritual teaches you a way to animate and bring a spirit into your poppet. Perform this ritual after the poppet is stuffed and ready to work.

POPPET LIFE RITUAL

This ritual is an essential part of making your poppet magic work effectively. This ritual gives life and spirit to your poppet, allowing it to work magic for you.

MATERIALS
- Incense based on magical need
- Charcoal disc and censer or incense burner
- Matches or lighter
- Completed poppet or doll

WORKING
1. Using the censer or burner and matches or lighter, light the incense. Pass the doll through the incense smoke, stating:

   Doll, I name thee (target's name). Anything I do to you happens to (target's name).

2. Exhale over the doll three times. After each exhale, state:

> *Doll, I give you life on this day. To thank
> me, do as I say.*

3. Now that the doll has life, you can start working
   the doll.

Apple-Head Dolls

One of the more unique poppet styles is the apple-head doll.
These dolls combine the magic of apples with ancestor veneration. This combination creates a potent spirit vessel for
your home.

In proper storage—a cool place away from moisture and
light—these dolls can last for decades. A friend of mine found
one they made as a child, which was more than 20 years ago.

APPLE-HEAD DOLL RITUAL

The following ritual is a two-part ritual. The first part
of the ritual can be done at Mabon, or the Autumn
Equinox. The second part of the ritual makes a wonderful Halloween, or Samhain, ritual addition. The
purpose of the ritual is to create a vessel that your
ancestors can reside in when they visit.

This ritual calls for ancestor incense. The recipe for this incense can be found in part 3.

PART 1 MATERIALS
- Ancestor incense (for ancestor offering)
- Charcoal disc and censer or incense burner
- Matches or lighter

- Large apple
- Apple peeler
- Paring knife

PART 1 WORKING

1. Use the matches or lighter and censer or burner to light the ancestor incense. Breathe in the scent, remembering your ancestors and loved ones.

2. Carefully use the apple peeler to peel the skin from the apple.

3. Remove the core from the apple.

4. Use the knife to carve the face of your doll in the apple. As you carve the face, focus on your memories of this ancestor. When the face has been carved, pass the apple through the incense and recite the ancestor prayer:

   > *Ancestors of mine, protect me each day.*
   > *Help me to find my way. From you may*
   > *blessings of prosperity and strength stay.*
   > *Blessed ancestors, I honor you this day.*

5. Extinguish the incense. Place the apple head in a cool, dark place to dry. The apple will take approximately four to five weeks to dry.

PART 2 MATERIALS

- Ancestor incense
- Charcoal disc and censer or incense burner
- Matches or lighter
- Cardboard cone

- 2 pipe cleaners
- 10-by-6-inch piece of felt or other fabric
- Scissors
- Hot glue gun and glue
- Carved, dried apple head
- 3 to 7 rice grains
- 2 black beads or small googly eyes
- Water or other liquid

PART 2 WORKING

1. Check on the apple you carved four to five weeks ago. The apple should have started to shrivel and shrink. There should be clear indentations where you carved the eyes and mouth. If the apple is firm and dry, you can begin the process of building the body.

2. Use the matches or lighter and censer or burner to light the ancestor incense. Recite the ancestor prayer:

   Ancestors of mine, protect me each day.
   Help me to find my way. From you may
   blessings of prosperity and strength stay.
   Blessed ancestors, I honor you this day.

3. Wrap the pipe cleaners around the cone to create arms. Wrap the fabric around the cone and arms to create clothes, cutting the fabric as necessary with the scissors. Use the hot glue gun and glue to glue the clothing in place.

4. Add the apple head to the cone, gluing it in place.

5. Glue the rice to the head as teeth and the beads or googly eyes as eyes. When everything is in place and the glue has dried, carefully pass the doll through the incense smoke, reciting the ancestor prayer again.

6. Place the doll on your ancestor or main altar. Give the poppet life, naming the poppet after either a specific ancestor or your ancestors in general.

7. Give an offering of the water or other liquid to your ancestor. If you are performing a Samhain ritual, continue with it.

8. When the ritual is over, thank your ancestor for attending the ritual and extinguish the incense. You can either dispose of the doll and create a new one every year, or you can keep the doll in storage.

Health & Wellness Poppet Spells

Poppet magic works especially well for healing magic. Since poppets are shaped like the target, you can direct the energy of the spell to specific points that need healing.

HEADACHE REMOVAL POPPET

Use this poppet to heal yourself or your target when dealing with chronic headaches that will not go away. Use this poppet in addition to any medication and other treatment methods.

MATERIALS

- Sewing needle
- Blue candle
- Lavender essential oil (for headache relief)
- Candle holder
- Matches or lighter
- 10-by-6-inch piece of blue felt or other fabric
- Scissors
- 2 feet of purple or blue thread
- ¼ cup fresh or dried lavender flowers (for headache relief)
- ¼ cup fresh or dried peppermint (for headache relief)
- ¼ cup fresh or dried rosemary (for pain relief)
- ¼ cup fresh or dried thyme (for pain relief)
- 5 pins

WORKING

1. Use the needle to carve "Headache Relief" into the candle. Anoint the candle from top to bottom with the lavender essential oil. Place the candle in the holder, use the matches or lighter to light it, and state:

   As the candle burns, headaches do not return.

2. Fold the felt or fabric in half. Cut out a human-shaped figure. Place the two pieces of fabric together. You can either place the two pieces of fabric right sides together for a more polished final poppet or right sides out. Either way works.

Remember that a professional-looking poppet is not at all required for the spell to work.

3. Thread the needle with the thread and stitch the two fabric pieces together as best you can. Sew until the body is about 70 percent sewn shut. As you sew the poppet, chant:

   Headache pain never more to reign.

   If the poppet is currently right sides in, turn it right side out through the remaining unsewn hole.

4. Fill the poppet with the herbs. As you add the herbs, repeat the same chant from step 3. When all the herbal material has been added, finish stitching the poppet closed.

5. Give the poppet life, and place it near the candle.

6. Rub the pins with the lavender essential oil. Stab the head of the poppet with the first pin, stating:

   Headache, go away. Here you can no longer stay.

7. Stab the second pin in the same area, stating:

   Pain of head, release. Now there be peace.

8. With the third pin, stab the head and state:

   Headache, I banish you. With your pain I am through.

9. Stab the fourth pin in the head, saying:

   Pain from the brain, no longer remain.

10. Take the fifth pin and stab the head one last time, stating:

    Pain of head, release. Let there now be peace.

11. Extinguish the candle.

12. Burn the candle for 5 minutes every day, and feed the poppet the lavender essential oil. Work the poppet until your regular headaches are no more. Dispose of the poppet.

Depression Relief Poppet

While this poppet is designed to help heal and relieve depression, it is not a cure. For severe depression, seek professional medical help. Only use this spell to supplement professional treatment.

MATERIALS
- 5 votive candle holders
- 3 pink votive candles
- 2 white votive candles
- Sewing needle
- 10-by-6-inch piece of blue felt or other fabric
- Scissors
- 2 feet of blue or purple thread
- Personal effects of your target such as hair, nails, and teeth (Photos and scraps of old clothes are good substitutes.)
- ½ tablespoon dried lavender (for happiness, healing)
- ½ tablespoon dried catnip (for happiness)
- ½ tablespoon dried red and pink rose petals (for love, self-love)

- ½ tablespoon dried sunflower petals (for hope, sunshine)
- ½ tablespoon dried marigold (for hope, sunshine)
- Matches or lighter

WORKING

1. Set the candle holders in the shape of a star.

2. Use the needle to carve one of the following in each candle: "Peace," "Joy," "Cheerfulness," "Love," and "Happiness."

3. Once a word is carved into each candle, place the candles in the candle holders with the two white candles across from each other and the pink candles in the other holders.

4. Fold the fabric in half. Use the scissors to cut out a human shape. Thread the needle with the thread, and sew the poppet, leaving the head open, chanting:

   Peace and happiness come stay. Depression banished today.

5. Fill the poppet with the personal effects and herbal material. As you add each herb, feel yourself being happier, at peace, and calm. Finish stitching the poppet. Place the poppet in the center of the 5 candles.

6. Using the matches or lighter, light the candle carved "Peace," stating:

   Candlelight brings peace tonight.

7. Light the candle where "Joy" is carved. State:

   Joy light, burn bright.

8. Light the candle where "Cheerfulness" is carved. State:

   Light of cheer, no darkness I fear.

9. Light the "Love" candle, stating:

   Precious love brings healing from above.

10. Light the candle carved "Happiness." State:

    Happiness, come to me. From depression I am free.

11. Hold your hands over the poppet. While you hold your hands, state:

    Candlelight, burning bright, brings me healing on this night.

12. Let the candles burn for 5 to 10 minutes. As the candles burn, feel each of the words you carved surrounding you and filling you with their raw, emotional power. After 5 to 10 minutes, extinguish the candles.

13. Light the candles in the same order daily until the candles are completely burned. Repeat the process, replacing the candles as needed, until the healing is complete. Then dispose of the poppet and candles.

ENHANCE CHANCES OF CONCEPTION POPPET

This spell is a charm to aid in female fertility and pregnancy. See the packet chapter for the male version. Use this spell as a supplement for medical actions. To prevent an unwanted pregnancy, have your partner's consent before creating this poppet.

MATERIALS
- 10-by-6-inch piece of green felt or other fabric
- Scissors
- 2 feet of white thread
- Sewing needle
- Personal effects of both prospective parents
- 1 tablespoon dried white oak bark (for fertility)
- 1 tablespoon dried raspberry leaves (for fertility)
- 1 tablespoon dried cornflower (for the divine mother, fertility)
- 1 tablespoon dried angelica root (for protection)
- 1 teaspoon dried mandrake root (for fertility)
- Rose quartz tumble (for love for the unborn child)
- Moss agate tumble (for fertility)

WORKING
1. Fold the fabric in half, and use the scissors to cut a human shape from the fabric. With the threaded needle, start stitching the poppet at one of the hips and stitch around the poppet, leaving an opening. If sewing with the right sides together, turn the poppet right side out.

2. Place the personal effects in the poppet and state:

   For (prospective parents' names) to conceive the child they wish to have.

3. Add the herbs, stating:

   To achieve fertility, to be able to fully conceive.

4. Place the rose quartz into the poppet, stating:

   For the love of the unborn child.

5. Add the moss agate, stating:

   For fertility and strength.

6. Finish stitching the poppet. Place the poppet under the couple's mattress. Keep the poppet there until the couple has conceived and the child is born. Dispose of the poppet.

Immune System Booster Poppet

This poppet is great to use during cold and flu season, especially if you have a lot of contact with the general public, because this spell works as a shield, protecting you from seasonal colds and flu. This spell uses both the medicinal and magical properties of the herbs to work.

MATERIALS
- Stuffed doll that you can connect to yourself or your target
- Knife
- Sewing needle

- 1 foot of blue thread
- Personal effects such as hair, nails, and teeth (Photos and scraps of old clothes are good substitutes.)
- Small bowl and spoon
- 2 tablespoons black peppercorns (for antiviral properties, protection, removal of illness)
- 1 tablespoon ground cayenne pepper (for antiviral properties, protection, removal of illness)
- 2 tablespoons dried elderberry (for antiviral properties, protection, removal of illness)
- 1 tablespoon ground ginger (for antiviral properties, protection, removal of illness)
- ¼ cup dried nettle leaves (for decongestion, healing and health, return and reversal)
- ¼ cup dried and crushed pine needles (for antiviral properties, healing and health, protection, removal of illness)
- Blue candle
- Candle holder
- Eucalyptus essential oil (for antiviral properties, protection, removal of illness)
- Tea tree essential oil (for protection)
- Matches or lighter

WORKING

1. Using the knife, make an incision down the center of the doll. Split the cut open and remove some stuffing. Set the stuffing aside; it will return to the doll later.

2. Add the personal effects to the doll. Give the doll life by telling the doll its job.

3. Use the spoon to mix the herbs in the bowl. While mixing the herbs, visualize a blue light emanating from the mixture. Direct the energy from your mind down your arms, through your hands, and into the bowl and herbs.

4. Add the herbal mixture to the doll.

5. Replace the stuffing. Use the needle and thread to stitch the doll closed. Hold your hands over the doll, visualizing a blue light flowing from your hands throughout the doll. As you hold this image, state:

> *Doll of me, protect me. From seasonal illness I am free.*

6. Use the needle to carve "Immune Boost" into the candle. Put the candle in the candle holder. Anoint the candle with the essential oils, stating:

> *Oil of tea tree, from illness protect me.*
> *Oil of eucalyptus tree, from illness protect me.*

7. Place the poppet near the candle. The candlelight should be able to reach the poppet. Use the matches or lighter to light the candle, saying:

> *By this candle's light, immune system boosted tonight.*

8. Visualize the poppet glowing blue and black. Blue to heal any illness, and black to protect from any illness. See any new illnesses being sent back without access to your body. Hold that image for as long as you can. When you can no longer hold

the image, release that energy into the poppet. Extinguish the candle.

9. Each evening for the next month, anoint and light the candle. For 5 to 10 minutes before bed, recite the following chant:

   By this candle's light, immune system boosted tonight.

   Replace the candle as needed, carving and anointing each candle before use.

10. At the end of the month, feed the poppet with the tea tree and eucalyptus oils. Keep the poppet going until cold or flu season passes. At the end of the season, open the poppet and remove the herbal material. Store until the next season.

GENERAL HEALING POPPET

This poppet spell does not target a specific ailment and is great for general, long-distance healing.

You can find the recipe for the healing oil blend in the resources section.

MATERIALS
- Sewing needle
- Blue candle
- Healing oil blend
- Candle holder
- Matches or lighter
- 2 10-by-8-inch pieces of blue felt or other fabric
- Scissors

- Personal effects of your target such as hair, nails, and teeth (Photos and scraps of old clothes are good substitutes.)
- ¼ cup dried marigold (for healing)
- ¼ cup dried lavender (for healing)
- ¼ cup dried peppermint or spearmint (for healing)

WORKING

1. Use the pin to carve "Healing" into the candle. Anoint the candle from bottom to top with the healing oil. Place the candle in the candle holder, and use the matches or lighter to light the candle, stating:

    Healing light, grant me your power tonight.

2. Put the two pieces of fabric together and use the scissors to cut out a human shape. Using the needle and thread, stitch the shapes together, leaving a small opening at the top of the head. As you sew the figures together, visualize a blue light flowing from the candle to the poppet, filling the poppet.

3. Place the personal effects and herbs in the poppet. As you add the materials, continue to use the healing chant from step 1. Once the poppet is full, finish sewing the poppet and place it in front of the candle. Name the poppet and give it life.

4. Visualize the light from the candle enveloping the poppet, then traveling from the poppet to your target and enveloping them with the healing light. Hold the visualization as long as you can. When

you can no longer hold the visualization, release that energy into the candle and extinguish it.

5. Once a week, feed the poppet with the oil and light the candle for 5 to 10 minutes. Continue to feed and work the poppet for as long as the healing boost is needed. When the healing work is done, thank the poppet and release it from its work by cutting its threads and letting the energy go free. Dispose of the materials as you see fit.

Love & Relationships

Poppets work well for relationship and family magic.

PET LOVE POPPET

Use this poppet to attract and bring the love of a pet into your life. This spell helps you find the right pet for you. For safety, perform this spell outside where you can safely burn the poppet.

MATERIALS
- Firesafe container
- Fire extinguisher or bowl of water
- Scissors
- 2 pieces of paper
- Pen
- Magazines with pictures of animals and pets
- ¼ cup dried catnip (for happiness)
- ¼ cup fresh or dried yellow and white rose petals (for friendship, love)

- Small bowl and spoon
- Brown votive candle
- Votive candle holder
- Pin, needle, or knife
- Matches or lighter

WORKING

1. Prepare your outdoor workspace by clearing away any fire hazards, placing the firesafe container, and readying the fire extinguisher or bowl of water.

2. Use the scissors to cut out the shape of an animal you want to keep as a pet from the paper. Write your name on one shape and draw a sigil to represent pet love on the other shape.

3. Go through the magazines and use the scissors to cut out images of pets. As you cut the images, see yourself having a pet. Know you will have such love soon.

4. Mix the herbs in the bowl.

5. Use the pin, needle, or knife to carve "Pet Love" into the candle. Place the candle in the candle holder. Use the matches or lighter to light the candle.

6. Use wax from the candle to seal the edges of the paper poppet together, leaving an opening for the magazine clippings and herbs.

7. Gather the images of pets. Place each image into the poppet lovingly. Between each image, add a pinch of the herbal mixture.

8. Once all of the herbal mixture and images have been added, use wax from the candle to seal the rest of the poppet.

9. Bring the poppet and candle outside. Place the poppet in the firesafe container, and use the candle to set the poppet on fire. As the poppet burns, chant:

   Fire burning bright, bring me a pet tonight.

10. Extinguish the candle.

11. When the poppet has finished burning and the ashes are cool, sprinkle the ashes at a crossroads.

Heal a Broken Heart Poppet

The goal of this spell is to heal your heart, allowing yourself to be open to new relationships.

MATERIALS
- 2 2-by-2-inch pieces of red felt or other fabric
- Scissors
- Sewing needle
- 2 feet of blue thread
- Mixing bowl and spoon
- ¼ cup dried yellow dock (to attract love)
- 2 tablespoons dried red rose petals (for love)
- 1 tablespoon dried yarrow (for love)

- ¼ tablespoon dried peppermint (for healing, peace)
- ¼ tablespoon dried lavender petals (for healing, love)
- ¼ tablespoon dried lemon balm (for healing, release of wounds)
- ¼ tablespoon lemon zest (for cleansing, love)
- Stuffed doll that looks like you or the target
- Red pin

WORKING

1. Place the two pieces of red fabric together, and use the scissors to cut out a large heart. Thread the needle and stitch up the heart. Leave a small space on one side to use as your opening. As you stitch the heart, say this chant three times:

   I heal this broken heart so that new love may start.

2. Use the spoon to mix the herbs in the bowl. While you mix the herbs, recite the same chant from step 1 five to seven times.

3. Use half of the herbal mixture to fill the heart. Finish sewing the heart.

4. Cut the doll where the heart would be. Tear the opening enough to add the remaining herbal mixture to the doll. Use the needle and remaining thread to sew the cut in the doll shut.

5. Use the red pin to secure the heart to the doll. As you pin the heart, put one hand on your heart and keep the other on the heart you just made.

Feel your heart healing and being welcome to new love. Hold the feeling and image for as long as you can. When you can no longer hold the image, break the connection, extinguish the candle, and walk away.

6. Every day for the next month, hold the poppet for 5 to 10 minutes. As you hold the doll, feel the energy flowing from the doll into you. Hold the image for as long as you can. When you can no longer hold the image, break the connection and walk away. Continue the daily work until you feel your heart is completely healed or a new relationship has started and you are confident in this relationship. Dispose of the heart in the trash. Remove the herbal components from the doll. The doll can be used in other work or tossed into the trash.

TRUE LOVE COMES TO ME POPPET

Use this spell to bring true love into your life. Do not target a specific person. Targeting a specific person turns this from love work to domination magic.

MATERIALS
- Firesafe container
- Fire extinguisher or bowl of water
- 4 pieces of red construction paper
- 4 pieces of paper
- Scissors
- Pen

- Pin, needle, or knife
- Red taper candle
- Candle holder
- Matches or lighter
- Small bowl
- 2 sprigs of fresh rosemary (for love)
- 2 tablespoons red rose petals (for love)
- 2 tablespoons ground cinnamon (for love)
- ¼ cup sugar (for attraction)

WORKING

1. Prepare your outdoor workspace by clearing away any fire hazards, placing the firesafe container, and readying the fire extinguisher or bowl of water.

2. Put the 4 pieces of construction paper together in a pile. Use scissors to cut out a human shape from the pile. Set the pieces aside. They will become two poppets later.

3. On one piece of paper, use the pen to write out your petition including details like hobbies, personalities, and interests. Rewrite the petition on two clean pieces of paper. Use the first copy of your petition to design a sigil.

4. On two of the human shapes, draw your sigil. On the third shape, write your name. On the last shape, write "My True Love." Put the shapes together so you have two paper poppets, each one with the sigil facing front and the words or your name facing back.

5. Use the pin, needle, or knife to carve the words "True Love" in the candle. Hold an image of you in your perfect relationship for as long as you can. Direct that image into the candle to charge the candle. Place the candle in the holder and use the matches or lighter to light it, stating:

> **Candle burning bright, bring me love that's true and right.**

6. Use the candle wax to seal the paper poppet pieces together, leaving the heads open. As you seal the pieces, chant:

> **A love that's new, a love that's true.**

7. Place a rosemary sprig on each clean petition. Roll the rosemary up in the petition paper. Place a roll in each poppet.

8. Use the spoon to mix the remaining herbs in the bowl.

9. Add half of the herbal mixture to each poppet. Seal the heads of the poppets with more wax, reciting the same chant from step 6. Place the poppets on opposite sides of the candle, about 3 feet away.

10. Every day for 5 to 10 minutes, light the candle and recite your chant while holding the image of you in your perfect relationship. As you release the image, move the poppets 3 inches closer together.

11. When both poppets reach the candle holder, take the poppets outside and burn them in a firesafe

container. Once the ashes have cooled, sprinkle the ashes at a crossroads near your home to send the message everywhere. Repeat the spell until you find the person you are looking for. When you find that relationship burn the poppets, and scatter the ashes at a crossroads one last time.

Road Opener & Block Buster Poppet Spells

Road opener and block buster spells are one way to work with poppets. What happens to the poppets, happens to the targets. It's sympathetic magic.

Block Buster Poppet

This spell works by removing blocks and opening the way to success in your life.

MATERIALS
- Yellow taper candle
- Sewing needle
- Candle holder
- Matches or lighter
- Small bowl and spoon
- 5 tablespoons crossroads dirt (to open doors in all directions)
- ¼ cup dried basil leaves (to remove spirits causing blocks)
- 10-by-6-inch piece of white fabric
- Scissors
- 2 feet of yellow thread

- Personal effect such as a lock of hair, tooth, or fingernail (A photo or scrap of old clothing is a good substitute.)
- ¼ cup dried lemongrass (to remove negativity)
- ¼ cup dried lemon balm (to remove negativity)
- ¼ cup salt (to neutralize forces against you)
- 5 pins, preferably with yellow and orange pin heads

WORKING

1. On two sides of the candle, use the needle to carve "Block Buster." Place the candle in the candle holder and use the matches or lighter to light the candle. As you light the candle, state:

   Candle burning bright, bust open blocks in our way tonight.

2. In the bowl, use the spoon to mix the crossroads dirt and the basil. Stir the mixture well. While stirring, recite the following chant five to seven times or until well mixed:

   I have the key to unlock the blocks.

3. Fold the fabric in half, and use the scissors to cut out two human shapes. Thread the needle, and stitch the poppet almost completely together, chanting:

   Blocks in our way, we overcome them today.

   If you sewed the poppet with the right sides of the fabric together, turn it right side out.

4. Add the personal effect to the poppet and give it life.

5. Add 1 tablespoon of the basil and crossroads mixture, stating:

   I have the keys to unlock the blocks.

6. Add the lemongrass, stating:

   To remove negativity known and unknown.

7. Repeat step 5.

8. Add the lemon balm, stating:

   To cleanse the way. Closed no door shall stay.

9. Repeat step 5.

10. Add the salt, saying:

    To neutralize the evil sent my way.
    This darkness shall not stay.

11. Repeat step 5, adding the remaining mixture.

12. Finish stitching up the poppet.

13. Stab the 5 pins into the poppet in a line from the groin to the head. Place the poppet in front of the candle and state:

    Candle burning bright, bust open blocks in our way tonight.

14. Stare into the candle flame and visualize an obstacle in your way falling down. When you can no longer hold onto the image of the obstacle breaking, remove one of the pins. Extinguish the candle.

15. For the next four days, repeat step 14. When all of the pins are removed, the blocks are gone.

16. Dispose of the poppet once you have achieved success in what you were trying to accomplish.

ROAD OPENER POPPET

Use this spell to open up new opportunities and possibilities. For best results, focus on new opportunities rather than overcoming specific blocks.

MATERIALS
- Yellow candle
- Sewing needle
- Candle holder
- Matches or lighter
- Pair of old socks
- Scissors
- 2 feet of yellow thread
- Personal effect such as a lock of hair, tooth, or fingernail (A photo or scrap of old clothing is a good substitute.)
- 6 tablespoons crossroads dirt (to open doors in all directions)
- 5 tablespoons *abre camino*, which is available at botanicas and hoodoo supply shops (to open roads)
- Small bowl
- Skeleton key, which can be found at a hardware store, or a key without a lock (to open doors)
- 1 tablespoon dried sage (for cleansing)
- 1 tablespoon dried pine needles (for cleansing, protection)
- 1 tablespoon salt (to absorb ill will, neutralize negativity)

WORKING

1. Use the needle to carve "Road Opener" into the candle. Place the candle into the holder and use the matches or lighter to light the candle. As the candle begins to burn, state:

   Candle burning today, your light shows the way.

2. Use the spoon to mix the crossroads dirt and abre camino together in a bowl. As you mix, state:

   To open the doors every way. New opportunities now to stay.

3. Recite the statement five to seven times or until the dirt and abre camino are well mixed.

4. Use the scissors to cut a human shape from the socks. Use the needle and thread to stitch the two pieces together. Start stitching with the left arm, leaving the head as an opening to stuff the poppet.

5. Add the personal effect to the poppet and give the poppet life.

6. Add 1 tablespoon of the crossroads dirt and abre camino mixture to the poppet. As you add the mixture, state:

   Roads open today. Chances and opportunities come to stay.

7. Place the skeleton key in the poppet and state:

   I place this key to open all doors for me.

8. Repeat step 6.

9. Add the sage to the doll and state:

   Clean the way. Negativity banished this day.

10. Repeat step 6.

11. Sprinkle the pine needles into the poppet. State:

    Pine for prosperity, bringing success to me.

12. Repeat step 6.

13. Add the salt to the doll and state:

    To neutralize all ill will. Negativity made to stand still.

14. Repeat step 6, adding half of the remaining dirt mixture. Sprinkle the remaining dirt around the candle holder's base.

15. Stitch up the rest of the poppet. Place the poppet in front of the candle, stating:

    Candle burning today, your light shows the way.

16. Visualize many new doors and roads opening in your life. See yourself having successful opportunities. Hold this image for 5 minutes. Extinguish the candle. Repeat daily until the candle burns out. When the candle is done burning, the doors are open. Dispose of the doll as you see fit.

Luck & Money Poppet

Use this poppet to protect your luck and bring you new opportunities for luck and money.

MATERIALS
- 10-by-8-inch piece of green felt or other fabric
- 10-by-8-inch piece of yellow felt or other fabric
- Scissors
- Sewing needle
- 2 feet of yellow, green, or gold thread
- Personal effect such as a lock of hair, tooth, or fingernail (A photo or scrap of old clothing is a good substitute.)
- Small bowl and spoon
- 1 tablespoon abre camino, which is available at botanicas and hoodoo supply shops (to open roads)
- 3 tablespoons dried yellow or orange marigold flowers (for money and to protect money)
- 4 whole allspice kernels (for luck, money)
- 1 tablespoon dried chamomile flowers (for luck)
- 2 tablespoons dried cinquefoil (to attract money, protect money, protect against money and luck hexes)
- 1 tablespoon dried goldenrod (for money)
- 2 tablespoons dried basil (for protection and to attract money and wealth, break blocks and curses)
- 8 inches of silver chain or wire
- Skeleton key, which can be found at a hardware store, or a key without a lock (to open doors)

WORKING

1. Put the pieces of fabric together, and use the scissors to cut out the shape of a human. Thread the needle, and stitch the two pieces together, leaving an opening along the side. If you sewed the poppet with right sides of the fabric together, turn the poppet right side out.

2. Add the personal effect and give the poppet life.

3. Put all the herbs in the bowl. Use the spoon to mix the herbs, reciting the following chant three to five times or until well mixed:

   Protect the path of opportunity, bringing luck and prosperity to me.

4. Pour the herbal mixture into the poppet. As you add the mixture, use your hands to get the blend throughout the poppet's body. Finish stitching the poppet closed.

5. Place the key on the chain or wire and put it on the poppet as a necklace. As you place the necklace, state:

   This is the key that opens the doors for me.

6. Place the poppet where it won't be disturbed and you will remember to work it daily. Every morning, work the poppet until you feel new roads and opportunities have come your way. As you work the poppet, chant:

   Protect the path of opportunity, bringing luck and prosperity to me.

7. Once new roads and opportunities have come your way, dispose of the poppet in a method you feel is appropriate. Cleanse the key for future magical work.

Hexes, Curses & Justice Work

The use of poppets in curses is iconic. That is why I saved this section for last. Working baneful magic must be taken very seriously. I engage in baneful magic only as a last resort, after trying everything else. There have been times when my own baneful magic backfired on me from a lack of consideration of the consequences of my actions.

Baneful magic is not something to use simply when someone has upset you or pissed you off. Acting rashly with baneful magic will backfire and cause havoc in your life. To avoid unnecessary negative consequences, carefully consider the following questions:

1. Could there be any background details to the situation that you may not be aware of?
2. Have you or the person you are doing the spell on behalf of done anything that might have brought about the situation leading to a need for baneful spellwork?
3. Can you live with the potential consequences of the spellwork? Is there a chance at all that you will regret casting your spell? When your spell works

and your target has started to receive treatment, can you live with the results that you are seeing?

4. Does casting the spell fit within your personal ethics and morals?

5. If the answers to questions 1 and 2 are "yes," take some time to reevaluate everything before casting the spell. For questions 3 and 4, if the answers are "no," do not cast the spell. Only cast baneful magic when you are 100 percent certain you can accept the consequences of actions and inactions and believe it to be morally and ethically the right thing to do.

To Harm a Relationship

This spell is for an unhealthy relationship that you want torn apart. The spell targets the toxic individual, allowing the other party to leave and enter healthy relationships. Make sure your information is accurate; otherwise, your relationships will suffer.

MATERIALS
- Firesafe container
- Fire extinguisher or bowl of water
- Black candle
- Rose thorn
- Mineral oil (for banishing, cursing, ill will)
- 2 tablespoons ground cayenne pepper (for heat, hexing, power)
- Matches or lighter
- Photo or drawing of your target

- Pen
- 1 teaspoon poppy seeds (for confusion)
- 1 teaspoon ground yellow mustard seed (for strife)
- 2 to 4 ounces clay

WORKING

1. Prepare your outdoor workspace by clearing away any fire hazards, placing the firesafe container, and readying the fire extinguisher or bowl of water.

2. Use the rose thorn to carve "Harm Relationship" into the candle. Anoint the candle with the mineral oil. Place the candle in the candle holder.

3. Sprinkle half of the cayenne pepper around the candle, stating:

   To cause ill will at fast speeds.

4. Use the matches or lighter to light the candle.

5. On the back of the photo or drawing, use the pen to write your target's name, their partner's name, and the words "Break Up." Light the paper or photo on fire from the candle. Place the burning paper in the firesafe container, and let it burn out. Extinguish the candle.

6. Add the remaining herbs to the cauldron, in any order, stirring between each herb. As you add each herb and stir, state:

   For the pain and suffering you have caused,
   all relationships with you are now on pause.

7. Once the herbs have been mixed well, begin to slowly mold and work the clay until it's malleable. Sculpt the clay into a human shape.

8. Use the rose thorn to dig a hole in the clay doll's heart.

9. Pour the herb mixture into the heart hole you created. If the mixture flows over and into the clay, work the remaining mixture into the clay, sealing the hole you made.

10. Use the rose thorn to scratch and tear at the heart. As you scratch and tear at the heart, repeat the following chant at least five times:

   Heartache is your fate. For your love is too late.

11. Set the poppet in front of the candle. Daily, as you pass the poppet, scratch some clay away, repeating the same chant from step 10.

12. When the relationship has ended, smash the poppet and throw away the debris. Your target can now have healthy relationships again.

GET MONEY OWED HEX

This spell is to receive money that you are owed from work. Use this spell to target employers who are late in paying your wages and when the lack of that money is causing you to have unnecessary hardships. For safety, perform this spell outside with water or a fire extinguisher nearby. If a firesafe container, such as a cauldron, is not available, burning the poppet on clear pavement or dirt should work.

MATERIALS

- Firesafe container
- Fire extinguisher or bowl of water
- Two pieces of paper
- Scissors
- Green pen
- Green candle, preferably a chime candle
- Matches or lighter
- 2 tablespoons mustard seeds (for discord, strife)
- 12 rose thorns (for relationship difficulties)
- 2 tablespoons dried nettle leaves (to hex, sting)
- 2 tablespoons dried galangal root (to return to sender)
- 2 tablespoons dried alfalfa (for money)
- 2 tablespoons dried poppy seeds (for emotional discord)
- Pin

WORKING

1. Prepare your outdoor workspace by clearing away any fire hazards, placing the firesafe container, and readying the fire extinguisher or bowl of water.

2. Stack the paper and use the scissors to cut two human shapes from it. On one shape, use the pen to write the name of your target. On the other piece, draw a sigil that represents your current situation.

3. Use the matches or lighter to light the green candle. Hold the two paper poppet pieces with the target's name and the sigil facing out. Use the wax from the candle to seal all but the poppet's head.

4. Fill the poppet with the herbs and finish sealing the poppet. Gently shake the poppet to distribute the herbs evenly throughout the body.

5. Give the poppet life.

6. Use the pin to stab the poppet's head twice and its heart once. With each stab, direct your distress into the poppet, transferring the problems your employer caused back to them. Recite each statement with the corresponding stab:

   Until to me you pay, emotional strife sent your way. **First stab.**

   To you I send emotional distress without rest. **Second stab.**

   When all is paid, all chaos will fade. **Third stab.**

7. Place the poppet in the fire safe container, and use the candle flame to set the poppet on fire. Let the poppet burn completely, and extinguish the candle. As the poppet burns, know that your employer will face everything you have faced recently until they pay you what's due. When their debt to you is paid, both of your lives will return to normal.

Stop a Cheating Partner

This spell is a way to release your pain and frustration when you find out that your partner has been cheating. Use this curse only when addressing and talking about the problem has not worked.

MATERIALS
- Clean, used underwear from your target or 2 10-by-8-inch pieces of red felt or other fabric
- Scissors
- Sewing needle
- About 30 inches of thread that matches the underwear or fabric
- 1 pinch ground cayenne pepper (to burn sexually, hex)
- 1 pinch rose thorns (to cause pain, prick in the side)
- 1 pinch saltpeter (to cause impotence)
- 1 pinch mustard seeds (for chaos, strife)
- 1 pinch masterwort (for domination)
- Mixing bowl and spoon
- Pin

WORKING
1. Use the scissors to cut the underwear into two human shapes. Thread the needle with the thread, and sew the two poppet pieces together, leaving an opening at the groin area, stating:

    For cheating on me, impotent you will be.
    No more sexual proclivity. Desire only me.

2. Use the spoon to mix the herbs and saltpeter in the bowl. As you stir the mixture, repeat the following chant three to five times or until well mixed:

   Desire and lust only for me, or have pain from engaging sexually.

3. Fill the poppet with the herb and saltpeter mixture. Use your hands to work the mixture into all of the poppet and sew up the groin area.

4. Hide the poppet under your bed or mattress near the foot of the bed. When you suspect your partner is cheating, stab the poppet in the groin area with the pin. Work the poppet until the cheating is admitted, the behavior stops, and the affair is dissolved. Dispose of the poppet in the trash away from your home.

ABUSE JUSTICE

This spell is to help you safely release your emotions after leaving an abusive relationship. Only use this spell after you are safe and well away from your target. This is a two-part spell.

PART 1 MATERIALS
- Mixing bowl
- Air-dry clay
- 2 tablespoons ground cayenne pepper (for fire, hexing, speed)

- 2 tablespoons ground galangal root (for justice, revenge and to return to sender)
- 1 tablespoon ground nettle leaves (for cursing, hexing, justice)
- 1 tablespoon dried woodruff (for overcoming adversaries)
- 5 pins
- Mineral oil (for banishment, cursing, hexing)

PART 1 WORKING

1. In the bowl, knead the clay and herbs together. As you knead the mixture, focus on the person who abused you. Direct your emotions into the clay.

2. Shape the clay into a human shape. Project the image of your abuser onto the clay. Name the clay poppet for your target and give it life.

3. Dip the pins in the mineral oil, and stab the clay doll with the pins. With each stab, state:

   For the abuse that you put me through, this curse I cast upon you.

4. Set the poppet somewhere safe to dry. It should take 36 to 48 hours for the clay doll to dry completely.

PART 2 MATERIALS

- Dried poppet
- Hammer
- Broom
- Trash bag

PART 2 WORKING

1. Take the dried poppet and the other materials outside. Use the hammer to smash the poppet into small pieces. With each slam of the hammer, feel your emotions release and your body become lighter.

2. Sweep up the smashed poppet. Toss what you swept up into the trash bag, stating:

    Into the trash, I place this part of my past.

3. Put the trash bag in a trash can. Walk away knowing that you are now free from that part of your past. You can now begin the healing process.

PART III
RESOURCES

Herbal & Root Correspondences

One of the main fillings used in container magic is herbs. In witchcraft and magical work, herbs refer to any and all plant matter, not just the herbs and spices you may be familiar with in your kitchen. The herbs in your kitchen are a powerful source of magic. The following list is an alphabetical list of a variety of herbs that you may wish to work with in your magical practices. This is not a complete list, but it will get you started.

Abre Camino: Banishment, opening roads, removal

Alfalfa: Drawing money, prosperity, protection

Allspice: Healing, luck, money

Aloe Vera: Love, peace in the afterlife, prosperity, protection, success

Angelica Root & Leaf: Angel work, divination, health, hex removal, meditation, protection

Arnica: Increasing psychic powers, protection from spirits

Avocado: Beauty, luck, lust

Banana: Empowerment, fertility, prosperity

Banana Leaves: Money spells, prosperity

Basil: Ancestral work, astral travel, attracting money, exorcisms, house blessings, invoking dragons, love, protection, rituals for the dead, wealth

Bay Leaf: Protection, psychic powers, purification, strength

Bearberry: Money, power, protection, strength, victory

Beet: Love magic

Bergamot: Clarity, money

Betony (Wood): Curse and hex breaking, protection, purification

Bilberry: Generating luck, generating wealth, protection

Birch: Protection, purification

Blackberry: Exorcisms, healing, money, protection, returning evil

Black-Eyed Susan: Channeling spirits, cleansing, connecting with the dead, grounding, integration, releasing

Black Peppercorns: Exorcisms, protection

Blueberry: Protection

Burdock Root: Protection, uncrossing

Calendula/Marigold: Health, money, prophetic dreams, prosperity, protection, psychic development

Cardamom: Love, lust

Catnip: Cat magic, break up spells, fertility, happiness, healing, legal matters, love, psychic powers, stopping spells

Cayenne Pepper: Fidelity, hex breaking, protection, removal

Cedar: Healing, money, protection, purification

Celery Seeds: Concentration, inducing sleep, lust, psychic powers

Chamomile: Luck, money, peace, protection, purification, sleep

Chervil: Joy, peace, spiritual growth, wisdom

Cinnamon: Consecration, love, lust, money, purification, sexuality, wealth

Cinquefoil (Five-Finger Grass): Attracting money, gambling luck, removing curses

Clover: Exorcisms, fidelity, love, money, protection, success

Cloves: Astral travel, exorcisms, love, protection, psychic abilities

Comfrey Leaf: Money, protection, safe travels

Coriander Seeds: Fidelity, healing, health, love, lust

Crab Apple: Fertility, healing

Cramp Bark: Luck, protection

Damiana Leaf: Attraction, divination, psychic abilities, psychic visions

Dandelion: Enriching, manifesting wishes, money, purification

Devil's Shoe String: Keeping away evil, luck, protection

Dill: Aiding sleep, bringing in luck, curse and hex breaking, passion

Echinacea: Making offerings to spirits, Strengthening spells

Elderberry: Exorcisms, healing, prosperity, protection

Eucalyptus: Breaking bad habits, protection from jinxes and curses, warding against evil

Eyebright: Mental powers, psychic powers

Fennel: Protection, psychic sight, purification

Fenugreek: Money

Feverfew: Protection, warding against disease

Figs: Divination, fertility, love

Galangal Root: Curses, hexes, justice work, money, protection, uncrossing

Garlic: Antitheft, exorcisms, lust, protection

Ginger: Love, money, power, protection, success

Ginkgo: Fertility, healing, mental clarity

Ginseng: Beauty, fertility, healing, lust, protection, sexuality, wishes

Goldenrod: Divination, money

Goldenseal: Healing, money

Honey: Attraction, love, money, slow work, stickiness, sweetness

Horseradish: Exorcisms, purification

Hyssop: Cleansing, protection, purification

Ivy: Healing, protection

Jasmine: Love, money, prophetic Dreams

Juniper: Exorcisms, love, protection

Knotgrass/Knotweed: Binding, health

Lavender: Happiness, healing, love, meditation, peace, protection, psychic abilities, purification

Lemon: Friendship, justice, love, purification

Lemon Balm: Cleansing, healing, love, success

Lemongrass: Lust, psychic powers, repelling snakes

Licorice: Fidelity, love, lust

Lime: Banishment, cleansing, clearing and cutting, energy, justice, protection, removal, souring

Lungwort: Attracting love, healing the lungs, making offerings to the gods of air, protection

Mace: Control, domination, love, lust, psychic development, sexual attraction

Masterwort: Control, domination, ownership

Meadowsweet/Queen of the Meadow: Divination, female domination, gambling luck, happiness, love, motherhood, peace, woman's power; counterpart to woodruff/master of the woods

Milk Thistle: Perseverance, strength, wisdom

Mugwort: Astral projection, prophetic dreams, protection, psychic powers, strength

Mullein: Courage, divination, exorcisms, love, protection

Mustard Seed: Biblical wisdom, confusion, discord, prosperity, strife, success

Nettle Leaf: Exorcisms, breaking jinxes, healing, lust, protection

Nutmeg: Fidelity, gambling luck, luck, money, prosperity

Oats: Money

Olives: Fertility, healing, lust, peace, protection

Onion: Exorcism, healing, lust, money, prophetic dreams, protection

Orange: Divination, money, love, luck

Oregano: Joy, keeping away the law, strength, vitality

Parsley: Fortune, healing, lust, protection, purification, success, underworld workings

Passionflower: Friendship, house Blessings, peace, sleep

Peppermint: Healing, love, psychic powers, purification

Pine: Cleansing, exorcisms, fertility, healing, money, protection, removing evil

Plantain: Healing, strength, protection

Poppy Seed: Altered states of consciousness, commerce, confusion, fertility, love, money, prosperity, trade

Quince: Happiness, protection, love

Radish: Lust, protection

Raspberry: Good luck, love, protection

Rose Hips: Love, luck

Rosemary: Cleansing, drawing the aid of spirits, healing, love, lust, mental focus, protection

Sage: Cleansing, consecrating, guarding against the evil eye (white sage), purification, spell reversal

Saint-John's-Wort: Divination, happiness, health, love, protection, strength

Salt: Absorbing and neutralizing energetic forces, cleansing, removal

Skullcap: Fidelity, love, peace

Sugar: Attraction, friendship, love, money, sweetening,

Thyme: Courage, good luck, healing, health, love, psychic powers, purification, sleep

Tomato: Love, lust, prosperity, protection

Turmeric: Purification

Valerian Root: Cleansing, curse and hex breaking, love, peace, protection, purification

Vinegar: Baneful magic, hexing, preservation, souring

Watercress: Dragon spirits, protection, purification

Willow Bark: Healing, love, protection

Witch Hazel: Chastity, protection

Woodruff/Master of the Woods: Male domination, male power, money, overcome adversaries, protection, strength, victory; counterpart of meadowsweet/queen of the meadow

Wormwood: Calling spirits, love, protection, psychic powers, underworld work

Yarrow: Courage, exorcism, love, protection, psychic development

Yellow Dock: Attracting customers, drawing love, drawing money

CRYSTAL, METAL & MINERAL CORRESPONDENCES

Many people who practice magic enjoy working with the energy of crystals and semiprecious stones. Like herbs, these items are common materials used in spells or rituals. Any rock, crystal, stone, mineral, or metal can be worked with magically, and this is a simple alphabetical list of common crystals and semiprecious stones that you can experiment with and add to your magical practices. Note that an asterisk indicates crystals that are not safe for use with water or other liquids.

Agate: Love, luck, mental clarity

Aluminum Foil: Protection, reflection, removal

*Amazonite: Dispelling negativity, encouraging universal peace and love

Amber: Fertility, luck, money, protection, success

Amethyst: Courage, dreams, happiness, healing, love, peace, psychic abilities

*Apatite: Drawing off negativity, promoting psychic and spiritual well-being

Aventurine: Eyesight, gambling luck, healing, luck, mental powers, money, peace

Bloodstone: Agriculture, business, courage, halting blood, healing, legal matters, strength, victory, wealth

Carnelian: Promoting peace, relieving depression, sexuality

*Celestite: Cleansing negativity, connection to spirit guides, stimulating psychic abilities

Citrine: Nightmare protection, protection, psychic abilities, success, warding off nightmares

Clear Quartz: Boosting any other crystals or herbs, healing, protection, psychic abilities, spirituality

Coffin Nail: Binding, curses or hexes, increasing potency of magic, protection

Diamond: Aids in sexual dysfunction, courage, creates sexual dysfuntion, healing, love, peace, protection, reconciliation, spirituality, strength

Emerald: Eyesight, exorcisms, love, mental powers, money, protection

*Fluorite: Mental powers

Garnet: Healing, protection, strength

*Gypsum: Cleansing and removal, good luck, protection

*Halite (Rock Salt): Purification, warding off evil

*Hematite: Divination, grounding, healing

*Iron Pyrite: Divination, luck, money

Iron Railroad Spikes: Baneful magic, binding, house protection

Jadeite: Healing, longevity, love, money, prosperity, protection, wisdom

Jasper: Healing, protection, returning negativity

Jet: Antinightmare, divination, health, luck, protection

*Labradorite: Happiness, peace, peace of mind, relaxation, tranquility

Lapis Lazuli: Courage, fidelity, healing, joy, love, protection, psychic abilities

*Malachite: Business success, love, peace, power, protection

Moonstone: Dieting, divination, gardening, love, moon goddess, protection, psychic abilities, protection, youth

Moss Agate: Fertility, gardening, happiness, long life, riches

Obsidian: Banishing, grounding, protection, removal

Red Jasper: Beauty and grace spells, curing fevers, healing, protection against poison, returning negativity

Rose Quartz: Attracting love, promoting happiness and peace, stimulating love

Ruby: Antinightmare, joy, power, protection, wealth

Saltpeter: Breaking jinxes, causing impotence, cleansing, turning luck around

Selenite: Absorbing and neutralizing energy, cleansing

Smoky Quartz: Grounding, overcoming depression

Snowflake Obsidian: Banishing, grounding, protection, removal

Sunstone: Energy, health, protection, sexual energy, sun god

Tiger's-Eye: Courage, divination, energy, luck, money, prosperity

*Turquoise: Healing, love, luck, protection, warding off psychic and spiritual attacks, wealth

MAGICAL PROPERTIES
OF LOCATIONS

Dirt is everywhere. One of the unique aspects of dirt is that it absorbs all the energy from the location you find it in. Working with dirt is working directly with the spirit of the land. There is power in urban locations, as well as natural, wild locations. This list gives some hints on how you might want to work with dirt in your own magical practice.

Airport: Moving, transportation, traveling

Army/Military Base: Protection

Bank/Credit Union: Anything related to finances, expenses, or money in your life

Bar/Tavern: Healing alcoholism, socialization, stopping drinking

Cemeteries: Ancestor work, baneful magic, energy of the dead

Church: Blessings of god, cursing, sacred energy

Courthouse: Justice work

Crossroads: Changes in life, force of change, sending energy in all directions

Desert: Banishment, decay, heat, hexing, removal, speed

Doctor's Office: Healing, sickness

Forests/Woods: Border between worlds, elves and fae, fear and haunting, fertility and life, protection

Home: Connection to your home, personal effect

Hospital: Beginnings, causing an illness, death, endings, healing

Mall: Commerce, meeting people, socialization, trade

Mountain: Ancient wisdom, clear sight, creating blocks, divination, protection

Ocean Coast: Attracting (high tide), cleansing, commerce, healing, money, removing (low tide), trade

Police Station: Baneful magic, justice work, protection

Pond: Cleansing, divination, healing, psychic development, underworld portals

River/Stream: Attraction and movement (flowing toward you), commerce, removal (flowing from you), trade

School/Library: Block busting, education, knowledge, mental focus, skill development, training

Stop Sign: Causing things to stop

CURIOS & OTHER MATERIALS

Curios are natural or human-made items that are used in spells and rituals for the symbolism they contain. Some curios are in the form of animal remains, and others are items like nails, mirrors, and keys. This alphabetical guide will help start you on your path to working with magical curios. Many of the following materials can be bought online, at hardware stores, or through Conjure or hoodoo supply shops.

Alligator Claw: Luck, money, success

Alligator Tooth: Attracting money, gambling luck, good luck

Cat Claw: Protection against evil

Cat Whisker: Balance, healing, luck

Coffin Nail: Binding, curses or hexes, increasing potency of magic, protection

Coyote Bone: Balance, cunning, intellect, luck, skill, strength

Crab Shell: Getting people to back off, reversing curses, hexes, and other spells

Dirt Dauber's Nest: Breakup work, business success, enemy work, money

Eggshell: Protection from hexes

Fire Ant: Bringing chaos, causing confusion, hot foot work

Iron Railroad Spikes: Baneful magic, binding, house protection

Magnet: Attraction, repelling

Mirror Fragment: Protection, reflection, removing, repelling, returning to sender

Nail: Cursing, protection, securing and stabilizing

Needle: Cursing, healing, health, pain, protection

Pin: Binding, cursing, pain, protection

Porcupine Quill: Baneful magic, bringing protection, causing pain

Rabbit's Foot: Good luck

Shed Snake's Skin: Banishment and removal, protection, rebirth and renewal

Skeleton Key: Locking and securing, opening and unlocking opportunities

Snail Shell: Slowing things down, stalling progress so you can catch up

Incense Recipes

To make incense you need only a few tools aside from the herbs: a mortar and pestle or small mixing bowl and spoon and an airtight storage container that can be kept in a dark, dry, and cool area. Start the process of mixing the incense by tapping into the herbal spirits and directing that energy.

While mixing the herbs in the mortar with the pestle or in the bowl with the spoon, direct your intent into the contents. Once it is well mixed, the incense is ready to burn. To use the incense, you will need a censer or heat pad and a charcoal disc. Use these incenses for power boosts and container food.

Ancestor Incense:
- 2 tablespoons dried angelica root (to attract spirits)
- 2 tablespoons dried basil leaves (to honor the dead)
- 2 tablespoons powdered or finely ground frankincense resin (to attract spirits)
- 2 tablespoons dried patchouli leaves (to honor the dead)

Astral Travel Incense:
- 2 tablespoons dried catnip (for mental powers, psychic gifts)
- 2 tablespoons dried marigold (for astral travel, psychic development)
- 2 tablespoons dried mugwort (for astral travel, meditation, psychic development)
- 2 tablespoons dried wormwood (for calling spirits, connection to underworld and spirit worlds, psychic abilities, spirit work)
- 2 tablespoon dried yarrow (for protection while in the spirit worlds, psychic development)

Career Success Incense:
- 2 tablespoons dried rosemary (for home needs)
- 2 tablespoons dried marigold (for luck, protection of money, success)
- 2 tablespoons dried pine needles (for fertility, money)

- 2 tablespoons powdered or finely ground dragon's blood resin (for money)
- 2 tablespoons ground nutmeg (for good fortune, luck, money, success)

Cleansing/Banishing Incense:
- 2 tablespoon dried basil: (for banishment, exorcisms, protection)
- 2 tablespoon powdered or finely ground frankincense resin (for banishment, protection, removal)
- 2 tablespoon dried pine needles (for cleansing, protection)
- 2 tablespoon dried sage (for blessings, cleansing, protection)
- 1 tablespoon dried rosemary (for cleansing, removal)

Fast Cash Incense:
- 2 tablespoons dried cinquefoil (for fast cash)
- 2 tablespoons ground cinnamon (for money)
- 2 tablespoons dried marigold (to protect money)
- 2 tablespoons dried pine needles (for long-term financial success)
- 2 tablespoons ground nutmeg (for money, wealth)

Healing Incense:
- 2 tablespoons dried angelica root (for health)
- 2 tablespoons ground black pepper (to banish ill health)

- 2 tablespoons dried galangal root (for fire, health, wellness)
- 2 tablespoons dried lavender (for health, wellness)
- 2 tablespoons dried pine needles (for healing, protection)

House Blessing Incense:

- 2 tablespoons powdered or finely ground frankincense resin (for blessing)
- 2 tablespoons dried lemon balm (for cleansing, blessing)
- 2 tablespoons dried rosemary (for home needs, protection, removal)
- 2 tablespoons dried sage (for blessing, cleansing)

Love & Lust Incense:

- 2 tablespoons dried rose petals (for love, lust, romance)
- 2 tablespoons dried patchouli leaves (for desire, passion, sexuality)
- 2 tablespoons dried lavender (for love, peace)
- 2 tablespoons dried cinnamon (for desire, lust, passion)

Peaceful Home Incense:

- 2 tablespoons dried catnip (for peace)
- 2 tablespoons dried chamomile (for peace)
- ¼ cup dried lavender (for peace)

- 3 tablespoons dried rosemary (for home needs, a peaceful home)
- 2 tablespoons dried peppermint (for peace, relaxation)

Protection Incense:

- 2 tablespoons dried angelica root (for protection)
- 2 tablespoons dried basil (for protection)
- 2 tablespoons powdered or finely ground dragon's blood resin (for protection)
- 2 tablespoons dried nettle leaves (for protection, returning to sender, reversal)

Psychic Development Incense:

- 2 tablespoons dried catnip (for psychic powers)
- 2 tablespoons dried ginkgo leaves (for clarity of thought)
- 2 tablespoons dried lavender (for mental powers, psychic gifts)
- 2 tablespoons dried marigold (for psychic development)
- 2 tablespoons dried mugwort (for psychic development)

OIL RECIPES

These infused oils add power to your spells and make great container foods.

To make the oils, you need a mason jar, herbs, a carrier oil, such as canola oil, cheese cloth, and a mixing bowl. Begin by adding the chosen herbs to the mason jar. Secure the lid and shake between each herb added to mix well. Once all the herbs have been added, fill the mason jar with the carrier oil. There should be a four-to-one ratio of oil to herbal material. Seal the jar, and shake the jar two times daily to mix the infusion. After four to six weeks, strain the oil into the bowl using the cheese cloth. Clean the jar, dispose of the herbs, and return the strained oil to the jar.

Left away from heat and direct light, these oils will last a year.

Banishing Oil:

- 2 tablespoons powdered or finely ground dragon's blood resin (for banishing)
- 2 tablespoons dried nettle leaves (for banishing, reversal)
- 2 tablespoons dried rosemary (for exorcism, protection)
- 1½ cups carrier oil

Cleansing Oil:

- 2 tablespoons dried angelica root (for banishing, removal)
- 2 tablespoons powdered or finely ground frankincense resin (for blessings)
- 2 tablespoons dried lemon balm (for cleansing, blessing, removal)
- 2 tablespoons dried pine needles (for banishment, protection, removal)
- 2 cups carrier oil

Healing Oil:

- 2 tablespoons dried allspice (for healing)
- 2 tablespoons dried lavender (for healing)
- 2 tablespoons dried lemon balm (for healing)
- 2 tablespoons dried marigold (for health, protect health)
- 2 tablespoons dried thyme (for general health, healing)
- 2½ cups carrier oil

Love Oil:

- 2 tablespoons dried rose petals (for romantic love)
- 2 tablespoons ground cinnamon (for love, lust, sexuality)
- 2 tablespoons dried lavender (for happiness, love, peace)
- 4 rose quartz tumbles or 2 tablespoons rose quartz chips (for romantic love, self-love)
- 1½ cups carrier oil

Money Draw Oil:

- 2 tablespoons dried pine needles (for prosperity, success)
- 2 tablespoons dried marigold (to protect money)
- 2 tablespoons dried basil (to attract money)
- 1½ cups carrier oil

Psychic Development Oil:

- 2 tablespoons dried ginkgo leaves (for clarity, mental focus)
- 2 tablespoons dried rosemary (for memory, mental focus)
- 2 tablespoons dried mugwort (for psychic development)
- 1½ cups carrier oil

Protection Oil:

- 2 tablespoons dried black pepper (for cleansing, protection from that which you remove, removal)
- 2 tablespoons powdered or finely ground dragon's blood resin (for protection)
- 2 tablespoons dried pine needles (for protection)
- 2 tablespoons dried galangal root (for justice work, protection, reversal)
- 2 tablespoons dried plantain leaves (for protection, strength)
- 2½ cups carrier oil

Spirit Offering Oil:

- 2 tablespoons dried angelica root (for calling to spirits, offerings to spirits)
- 2 tablespoons dried basil (for attracting the aid of spirits, offerings to spirits)
- 2 tablespoons powdered or finely ground frankincense resin (for blessings, offerings to spirits)
- 2 tablespoons powdered or finely ground myrrh resin (for connections to spirits, consecrating)
- 2 tablespoons dried wormwood (for connections to spirit, offerings to spirits)
- 2½ cups carrier oil

CONCLUSION

Container magic is by far my favorite form of magic to work, and one of the reasons I wrote this book was to share this love with you. The discovery of container magic changed my life and helped me reclaim my power. It is my hope that after reading this book, you will be able to take your magical work to the next level.

I hope that the skills I have shared with you enhance your practice of magic. You can apply much of the information to other forms of magic and spellwork as well to create a wide variety of magical works in your own style. Folk magic is the power of the people; use the spells in this book to reclaim that power and take charge of your life.

May your magic be effective, and may you claim your power. Good luck on your journey.

Acknowledgments

First off, I want to acknowledge and thank my agent, Bill Gladstone, for helping me find the publisher for this book and supporting me from the beginnings of this project.

Secondly, I want to acknowledge and thank Judika Illes, who helped me gain the confidence to submit my book after the first two publishers declined my proposal.

Thirdly, I would like to thank Heather Greene (my editor) and the rest of the staff at Llewellyn for making this dream become a reality.

Fourthly, I would like to thank my beta readers for helping me edit and work through my second draft: Kenya Coviak, Stephanie Lowe, Lori Brundige, Shawn Robbins, and Linda Bedell. Your suggestions and input helped this book transform from a good concept into a polished manuscript.

Finally, I thank my loving husband, Ben Weston, for all his support. He kept me grounded and focused while I worked. He was by my side from when this book began as a small concept to where it is now. I could not wish for a better or more supportive partner.

APPENDIX I
Exercises, Rituals & Spells in Order of Appearance

This book is full of rituals and exercises. Every chapter is so full it can be easy to lose track of where you found a spell. Use this list to find spells and rituals as they occur in the text.

Part I: The Basics

Choosing Your Container

Part II: Spells & Magical Works

Bottle Spells

Ball Spells

Box, Tin & Chest Spells

Sachet & Charm Bag Spells

Packet Spells

APPENDIX II
Spells by Need

One good thing about spell books is that they always contain a variety of ways to work magic. In this section, the spells and rituals have been listed by intent. Some spells fit into multiple categories, and you will find the spell in any category that it fits in.

Ancestor Veneration

Baneful & Justice Magic

Banishment & Removal

Block Busting & Road Opening

Cleansing

Curse Breaking & Curse Removal

Divination

Family & Home

Fertility

Health, Healing & Wellness Magic

Love, Lust & Romantic Relationships

Luck

Mental Health Assistance Work

Miscellaneous

Money

Protection

Psychic Development & Psychic Gifts

Recommended Reading

Backwoods Shamanism: An Introduction to the American Folk-Magic of Hoodoo Conjure and Rootwork by Ray "Doctor Hawk" Hess

Backwoods Witchcraft: Conjure & Folk Magic from Appalachia by Jake Richards

Basic Magick: A Practical Guide by Phillip Cooper

The Big Book of Practical Spells: Everyday Magic That Works by Judika Illes

The Big Little Book of Magick: A Wiccan's Guide to Altars, Candles, Pendulums, and Healing Spells by D. J. Conway

Blackthorn's Botanical Magic: The Green Witch's Guide to Essential Oils for Spellcraft, Ritual & Healing by Amy Blackthorn

The Book of English Magic by Philip Carr-Gomm and Richard Heygate

The Candle and the Crossroads: A Book of Appalachian Conjure and Southern Root Work by Orion Foxwood

The Casting of Spells: Creating a Magickal Life through the Words of True Will by Christopher Penczak

A Compendium of Herbal Magick by Paul Beyerl

The Complete Book of Incense, Oils & Brews by Scott Cunningham

The Conjure Workbook Volume 1: Working the Root by Starr Casas

Crossroads of Conjure: The Roots and Practices of Granny Magic, Hoodoo, Brujería, and Curanderismo by Katrina Rasbold

Cunningham's Encyclopedia of Crystal, Gem & Metal Magic by Scott Cunningham

Cunningham's Encyclopedia of Magical Herbs by Scott Cunningham

Cunningham's Magical Sampler: Collected Writings and Spells from the Renowned Wiccan Author by Scott Cunningham

Earth, Air, Fire & Water: More Techniques of Natural Magic by Scott Cunningham

Earth Power: Techniques of Natural Magic by Scott Cunningham

Encyclopedia of 5,000 Spells: The Ultimate Reference Book for the Magical Arts by Judika Illes

Everyday Magic: Spells & Rituals for Modern Living by Dorothy Morrison

The Flame in the Cauldron: A Book of Old-Style Witchery by Orion Foxwood

Folk Witchcraft: A Guide to Lore, Land, and the Familiar Spirit for the Solitary Practitioner by Roger J. Horne

Hoodoo Bible Magic: Sacred Secrets of Scriptural Sorcery by Miss Michaele and Professor Charles Porterfield

Hoodoo Herb and Root Magic: A Materia Magica of African-American Conjure by Catherine Yronwode

Introduction to Southern Conjure by Orion Foxwood

The Little Book of Curses and Maledictions for Everyday Use by Dawn Rae Downton

Magical Herbalism: The Secret Craft of the Wise by Scott Cunningham

The Magical Power of the Saints: Evocation and Candle Rituals by Rev. Ray T. Malbrough

Magic's in the Bag: Creating Spellbinding Gris Gris Bags & Sachets by Jude Bradley and Chere Dastugue Coen

Magic When You Need It: 150 Spells You Can't Live Without by Judika Illes

The Master Book of Herbalism by Paul Beyerl

Old Style Conjure: Hoodoo, Rootwork & Folk Magic by Starr Casas

Papa Jim's Herbal Magic Workbook: How to Use Herbs for Magical Purposes, an A–Z Guide by Papa Jim

Powers of the Psalms by Anna Riva

Practical Magic for Beginners: Techniques & Rituals to Focus Magical Energy by Brandy Williams

Practical Solitary Magic by Nancy B. Watson

Rootwork: Using the Folk Magick of Black America for Love, Money, and Success by Tayannah Lee McQuillar

The Secret Keys of Conjure: Unlocking the Mysteries of American Folk Magic by Chas Bogan

Southern Cunning: Folkloric Witchcraft in the American South by Aaron Oberon

Spells and How They Work by Janet Farrar and Stewart Farrar

True Magick: A Beginner's Guide by Amber K

Utterly Wicked: Hexes, Curses, and Other Unsavory Notions by Dorothy Morrison

The Witch's Bag of Tricks: Personalize Your Magick & Kickstart Your Craft by Melanie Marquis

A Witch's World of Magick: Expanding Your Practice with Techniques & Traditions from Diverse Cultures by Melanie Marquis

The Witch and Wizard Training Guide by Sirona Knight

Working Conjure: A Guide to Hoodoo Folk Magic by Hoodoo
Sen Moise

BIBLIOGRAPHY

Catholic Online. "St. Peter." Accessed February 25, 2022. https://www.catholic.org/prayers/prayer.php?p=186.

Crowley, Aleister. *Magick in Theory and Practice*. Eastford, CT: Martino Fine Books, 2011. https://www.sacred-texts .com/oto/aba/defs.htm.

Jesuit Resource. "Prayer to Saint Christopher." https:// www.xavier.edu/jesuitresource/online-resources /prayer-index/catholic-prayers.

St. Michael the Archangel Roman Catholic Church. "Prayer to St. Michael the Archangel." https:// saintmichaelcc.org/prayer-to-st-michael-the-archangel.

Three Initiates. *The Kybalion: A Study of the Hermetic Philosophy of Ancient Egypt and Greece*. CreateSpace, 2017.

Notes

Notes

Notes

To Write to the Author

If you wish to contact the author or would like more information about this book, please write to the author in care of Llewellyn Worldwide Ltd. and we will forward your request. Both the author and publisher appreciate hearing from you and learning of your enjoyment of this book and how it has helped you. Llewellyn Worldwide Ltd. cannot guarantee that every letter written to the author can be answered, but all will be forwarded. Please write to:

Charity Bedell
⁒ Llewellyn Worldwide
2143 Wooddale Drive
Woodbury, MN 55125-2989

Please enclose a self-addressed stamped envelope for reply, or $1.00 to cover costs. If outside the U.S.A., enclose an international postal reply coupon.

Many of Llewellyn's authors have websites with additional information and resources. For more information, please visit our website at http://www.llewellyn.com.